LOVE, LABOUR AND LIBERTY:

the eighteenth-century Scottish lyric

LOVE, LABOUR AND LIBERTY:

the eighteenth-century Scottish lyric

edited by

Thomas Crawford

A CARCANET PRESS PUBLICATION

First published 1976
by Carcanet Press Limited
266 Councillor Lane
Cheadle Hulme, Cheadle
Cheshire SK8 5PN

This book is published in co-operation with the Universities Committee on Scottish Literature and the Scottish Arts Council.

Printed in Great Britain
by W & J Mackay Limited, Chatham
by photo-litho

CONTENTS

PREFACE

The poems in this collection are the outcome of a song culture created and enjoyed in the eighteenth century by the people of lowland Scotland, from the farming classes in the countryside to the legal aristocracy in the city. The songs were as much the foundation of the contemporary poetic revival as any anti-quarian borrowings from the medieval makars, and they make use of English and Irish subjects and tunes as well as those that can justly be termed Scots. Of the three thousand or so songs published in Scottish poetical miscellanies and song-books from 1682 to 1785, some two thousand are in English, including many by Englishmen; and in the broadsides and chapbooks printed in Scotland for mass consumption during the century, about half the tales and songs seem to have been on English or Irish topics.

Scotland was as much a nest of singing birds as Elizabethan England is reputed to have been. The popular lyric tradition had two social functions − it transmitted past attitudes and emotions (some of 'folk' origin, some urban-plebeian, some upper class and even, ultimately, courtly) to the younger generation, and it provided a medium in which people of all ages could share such experiences as love, tragic emotion, 'social glee' and bacchanalian abandon, whether at the refined tea-table, at *celidhs* or 'rockins' round the farmer's ingle, or in all-male social clubs. Moreover, the popular medium was *used*, sometimes by dedicated writers like Ramsay and Burns, sometimes by quite ordinary people, to render experiences new in some degree, however slightly these might differ from what was felt by those around them or by those who went before them. And it could also be employed to further a cause, or for political or social satire. The lyric was a product of society; it served social life at every level; and it was, from the beginning of the century to the end, above all a poem to be *sung*.

The concept of individual authorship is not always the best approach to the lyrics of eighteenth-century Scotland, if only because so many of them are anonymous. For that reason I have arranged them according to type, subject-matter and theme in order to illustrate both their function and their range. The first two sections feature the folk and broadside modes; sections three, four, five and six are self-explanatory. We may perhaps define a folk-song as a song current among the members of some national, tribal, regional, urban, village, occupational or other community or group, transmitted orally from one generation to another, and subject to the laws that govern oral transmission — namely, the coexistence for long periods of a fixed norm with spontaneously occurring variation. And we may describe broadside or stall songs as songs with a considerable narrative content, generally fairly long, and often showing signs of sheer padding — they are the popular art form of the towns, and in their concern with crime and scandal as well as in their sometimes narrow moralism they anticipate the sensationalism and opinionated didacticism of the modern popular press.

Most lyrics of all nations and centuries are love poems, and Scotland is of course no exception. The second part of this book shows in how many different ways Scottish men and women felt and thought about love. Tenderness, sensuality, passion, lust, pathos, tragedy, humour, simplicity and artificiality — all are here, shared by lovers of every social class. Many of the best lyrics are those where the singer is a woman; they cannot easily be surpassed for delicacy or psychological acumen. Truly, lyrics of the kind printed here must have provided a regular schooling in sentiment for the young men and women of the century; being themselves 'the music of the heart,' they taught all lowland hearts to feel.

Every type of eighteenth-century song was used by Burns in his work as collector, refurbisher and creator of Scottish songs. It is therefore appropriate that most sections of the anthology should end with one or more songs by Burns, thus showing his relation to the popular culture which he both imitated and transcended.

I have allowed the lyrics to speak for themselves, without explanatory notes or a long critical introduction, so as not to overlap with my forthcoming study of Burns and the popular lyric. Because almost all the lyrics were in the first instance meant to be sung, it is hoped to publish a smaller selection, with the tunes, if there is sufficient demand from singers, students and folk-clubs, in Britain and America. In any case, I have tried to show in the table of lyrics as printed where their tunes can most easily be found. I have made some attempt to modernize the text by suppressing unnecessary capitals and italics, expanding contractions and rationalizing punctuation, but I have not aimed at a consistent spelling for the volume as a whole. Some eighteenth-century Scots spelling may be a guide to the author's or printer's pronunciation, for example, bonie (boany), bonnie (bawny), gude (gud or gweed), guid (gid), though it is often hard to tell what is intended when such words are differently spelt in successive stanzas of the same poem. In such matters as 'accidentals' I have kept in mind the needs of the general reader, for whom this book is intended.

Acknowledgements are due to the E.A. Hornel Trust for permission to reproduce songs from the St Clair (Mansfield) Manuscript, to the British Library Board and the Trustees of the National Library of Scotland for materials in broadsides and manuscripts held by the British Museum and the National Library of Scotland respectively, and to the Yale Editions of the Private Papers of James Boswell and the McGraw—Hill Book Company for the song 'Cut him down, Susie', copied or written by Boswell.

Aberdeen, March 1976   Thomas Crawford

Part I — The Life of the Nation

1   The Wren

The wren she lies in care's bed,
    In care's bed, in care's bed,
The wren she lies in care's bed,
    In mickle dule and pine, O,
When in cam Robin Redbreist,
    Redbreist, Redbreist,
When in cam Robin Redbreist
    Wi' succar-saps and wine, O.

'Now, maiden, will ye taste o' this,
    Taste o' this, taste o' this,
Now, maiden, will ye taste o' this?
    It's succar-saps and wine, O.'
'Na, ne'er a drap, Robin,
    Robin, Robin,
Na, ne'er a drap, Robin,
    Gin it was ne'er so fine, O.'

'And where's the ring that I gied ye,
    That I gied ye, that I gied ye?
And where's the ring that I gied ye,
    Ye little cutty quine, O?'
'I gied it till a sodger,
    A sodger, a sodger,
I gied it till a sodger,
    A kind sweet-heart o' mine, O.'

dule – woe; *pine* – pining; *succar-saps* – pap sweetened with sugar; *gied* – gave;
cutty – short in stature, and perhaps of temper; *sodger* – soldier.

2   When I was a wee Thing

When I was a wee thing
And just like an elf,
A' the meat that e'er I gat
I laid upon the shelf.

The rottens and the mice
They fell into a strife,
They wadnae let my meat alane,
Till I gat a wife.

And when I gat a wife
She wadnae bide therein,
Till I gat a hurl-barrow
To hurl her out and in:
The hurl-barrow brake,
My wife she gat a fa',
And the foul fa' the hurl-barrow,
Cripple wife and a'.

She wadnae eat nae bacon,
She wadnae eat nae beef,
She wadnae eat nae lang-kale
For fyling o' her teeth,
But she wad eat the bonie bird
That sits upon the tree;
Gang down the burn, Davie love,
And I sall follow thee!

a' – all; *gat* – got; *rottens* – young rats; *wadnae* – would not; *hurl* – wheel; *foul fa*
– evil betide; *lang-kale* – coleworts; *fyling* – soiling; *gang* – go; *sall* – shall.

3   The Nurse's Song

How dan, dilly dow,
How den dan,
Weel were your minny,
An ye were a man!

Ye wad hunt and hawk
And ha'd her o' game,
And water your dady's horse
I' the mill-dam.

How dan, dilly dow,
How dan flow'rs,
Ye's lie i' your bed
Till eleven hours.

If at eleven hours
Ye list to rise,
Ye's ha your dinner
Dight in a new guise.

La'rick's legs
And titlins' toes
And a' sic dainty
My manie shall hae.

dow – dove; *weel* – well; *minny* – mother; *an* – if; *ha'd* – hold; *ye's* – you shall; *list* – desire; *dight* – prepared; *la'ricks* – larks; *titlins* – titlarks.

4 The Quaker's Wife

The quaker's wife sat down to bake
And a' her bairns about her;
Ilk ane got their quarter cake,
The miller got his mouter.
Merrily merrily merrily merrily,
Merrily danced the quakers;
Merrily danced the quaker's wife,
And merrily danced the quakers.

a' – all; *ilk* – each; *quarter cake* – 'the fourth part of a round of oatcakes, the triangular portion thus cut' (*Scottish National Dictionary*); *mouter* – multure.

5 All in the Week's Work

On Saturday my wife she died
On Sunday she was buried
On Monanday I courted a wife
On Tuesday I was married
On Wednesday I stealt a horse
On Thursday I was apprehended
On Friday I was condemn'd to die
On Saturday I was hanged.

[There is no title in the source.]

Jock and Meg, Jock and Meg
Jock and Meg and Gam;
O was na she a clever lass,
She raid upon a ram.
She saddled it, she bridled it
As gin she had been a man;
She laid a leg in ilka side
And lap out o'er the dam.

na – not; *raid* – rode; *gin* – if; *ilka* – each; *lap* – leapt.

7   Bonnyness and Prettyness

Bonnyness gaed to the water to wash,
And Prettyness gaed to the barn to thresh;
Gae tell my master to pay me my fee,
For Prettyness winnae let Bonnyness be.

gae – go; *winnae* – won't.

8   Bonny Ann

Where will bonny Ann lie,
Where will bonny Ann lie,
Where will bonny Ann lie,
    I' the cauld nights o' winter?

Where but in the hen bauks
Where but in the hen bauks
Where but in the hen bauks
    Amang the rotten timmer, O?

There shall bonny Ann lie
There shall bonny Ann lie
There shall bonny Ann lie
    Till the warm nights o' simmer.

Wha d'ye think will cuddle her
Wha d'ye think will cuddle her
Wha d'ye think will cuddle her
   A' the cauld nights o' winter, O?

Wha but Patie o' the glen
Wha but ·Patie o' the glen
Wha but Patie o' the glen
   Will cuddle bonnie Annie, O!

hen bauks – hen loft; *timmer* – timber; *Patie* – Peter.

9   Willie Buckthorne

Willie Buckthorne had a cow,
They ca'd her Killiecrankie;
She fell o'er the auld-bane dyke
And broke her covenantie.

Hinck, spinck, sma' drink
Het yill and brandie;
Round about the haystack
Seeking houghmagandie.

Killiecrankie – battle (1689) between Jacobites and William III's forces; *covenantie* –
humorous euphemism from 'covenant', a key term in Scottish religious and political
history; *auld-bane* – old bone; *het* – hot; *yill* – ale; *houghmagandie* – sexual inter-
course.

10   Jacky Latin

There was a pretty maiden and she was dress'd in satin
And she was dress'd in satin,
And she sat down upon the ground
Cried – 'Kiss me Jacky Latin.
Kiss me Jacky, kiss me Jacky,
Kiss me Jacky Latin!
Won't you kiss your pretty maid,
Altho' she's dress'd in satin?'

THE FOLK MODE   17

11   I'd rather hae a Piece

I'd rather hae a piece as a kiss o' my jo,
I'd rather hae a piece as a kiss o' my jo,
I'd rather hae a piece as a kiss o' my jo,
And I'm easy whether I get him or no.

piece – smack; *jo* – sweetheart.

12   Cutty's Wedding

Busk and go dearie go,
Busk and go to Cutty's wedding;
Busk and go dearie go,
Busk and go to Cutty's wedding.
Cutty is a bonny lad
And he has a little wifie,
He'll gae to the town his lain
When she taks ony fickie-fyckie.

Busk and go dearie go,.
Busk and go to Cutty's wedding;
Busk and go dearie go,
Busk and go to Cutty's wedding.
Dadie says he winnae gae
Mammie says she was nae bidden;
I'll put on my ruffled cuffs
And slide awa to Cutty's wedding.

Cutty – Shorty; *busk* – dress; *his lain* – on his own; *fickie-fyckie* – petty fit of
temper; *winnae* – won't; *bidden* – asked.

13   Mally Lee

Mally Lee came down the street, her capuchin did flee;
She gae a look back again to see her negligee –
And we're a' going east and west, we're a' going ajee;
We're a' going east and west to court Mally Lee.

'What will ye gie me goodwife and what will ye gie me,
And what'll ye gie me goodwife and I'll court Mally Lee?'
'There's ten pound in my purse, there's ten pound and three —
There's ten pound in my purse gif ye'll court Mally Lee.'

'What'll ye gie me goodwife and what'll ye gie me mair,
What'll ye gie me goodwife an I'll court Mally Lee?'
'I'll gie ye the good gray yad that rides to the fair
I'll gie ye the good gray yad, gif ye'll court Mally Lee.'

As ye come in by Swinton and in by Swinton Kirk,
O there ye'll ken the bony lass by the biting of her lip.
And we're a' going east and west, we're a' going ajee,
We're a' going east and west to court Mally Lee.

capuchin — 'a female garment, consisting of a cloak and hood, made in imitation of
the dress of Capuchin friars' (Dr Johnson); *gae* — gave; *a'* — all; *ajee* — awry; *gie* —
give; *an* — if; *gif* — if; *mair* — more; *yad* — jade; *ken* — know.

14   The Tailor fell through the Bed

The tailor fell through the bed, thimbles an' a',
The tailor fell through the bed, thimbles an' a';
The sheets they were thin an' the blankets were sma',
An' the tailor fell through the bed, thimbles an' a'.

a' — all.

15   Tom o' Lin

Tom o' Lin and his wife and his good mither,
They gaed a' to the midden the gither;
Some shat thick and some shat thin —
'I'se for a spoon,' quo' Tom o' Lin.

Tom o' Lin's daughter she stood on the stair:
'O', quo' she, 'father, am I nae fair —
There's mony ane married wi' a far dinner skin.'
'The Deel tire ye out,' quo' Tom o' Lin.

THE FOLK MODE   19

Tom o' Lin's daughter she stood on the brig:
'O', quo' she, 'father am I nae trig?'
The brig it brake and she fell in —
'Your tochergude's paid,' quo' Tom o' Lin.

good mither — mother-in-law; *gaed* — went; *a'* — all; *the gither* — together; *I'se for* — I shall reach for; *ane* — one; *dinner* — darker; *Deel* — devil; *brig* — bridge; *trig* — spruce; *tochergude* — dowry.

16   Jenny's a' wet

Jenny's a' wet, poor body
Coming frae the kye;
Jenny's a' wet, poor body,
Coming frae the kye.
She draggled a' her petticoat,
She draggled a' her petticoat,
She draggled a' her petticoat,
And Jenny's never dry.

a' — all; *kye* — cows.

17   Comin thro' the Rye

Comin thro' the rye, poor body,
    Comin thro' the rye
She draigl't a' her petticoatie,
Comin thro' the rye!

Chorus
Oh Jenny's a' weet, poor body,
    Jenny's seldom dry:
She draigl't a' her petticoatie
    Comin thro' the rye.

Gin a body meet a body
    Comin thro' the rye,
Gin a body kiss a body
    Need a body cry?
    Oh Jenny's a' weet, etc.

Gin a body meet a body
  Comin thro' the glen
Gin a body kiss a body
  Need the warld ken!
   Oh Jenny's a' weet, etc.

Robert Burns

gin – if; *warld* – world; *a'* – all.

18   The Last Farewell and Lamentation of Mrs. McLeod
who was executed in the Grass-Market of Edinburgh on
the 8th of March, 1727, for the Crime of Forgery.

My loving husband he is gone
    And left me here forlorn,
Because for forgery I am seiz'd —
    Which makes my heart to mourn.
I never forgèd in my life,
    Nor knew what it did mean,
I never could include my heart
    To act such horrid sin.

But yet I apprehended was
    And cast in prison strong
For forgery, which grieves my heart;
    But those that did me wrong,
I leave them to the Judgment Day
    When they must all appear
To answer for my blood, when shed,
    Was purchasèd so dear.

When that the noble Lords did call
    I pannel'd was with speed,
The City Guard convey'd me there,
    To answer for the deed.
I chargèd was with forgery,
    Which still I did deny,
But I was guilty found at last,
    For which I'm doom'd to die.

Now all good people young and old
    Mark well what I shall say;
Serve ye the Lord while you have breath
    Sincerely night and day.
And never let your thoughts incline,
    To forgery be not bent,
For which I am arraign'd and cast:
    You'll see my fatal end.

Now fare you well all earthly joys,
    Farewell, farewell to thee;
My precious soul is pining long
    The Heavenly Courts to see.
O save me now in my distress,
    With thee there's joys full store;
Farewell, farewell all earthly joys,
    Farewell for evermore.

The Last Farewell — this is the second part of a broadside in the National Library of Scotland. Ry.IIIa.10 (108); *pannel'd* — was indicated.

19   Cut him down, Susie

Cut him down, Susie:
Haste ye wi' your gully knife —
Ye'se get him for your ain gudeman,
Gin ye contrive to save his life.

Cut him down and tak him hame
And send for folk to dance and sing,
And pit your arms about the neck
That on the gallows tree did hing.

James Boswell

gully — large knife; *ye'se* — you shall; *ain* — own; *gudeman* — husband; *gin* — if; *folk*
— people; *hing* — hang.

20   The Roving Maids of Aberdeen

The roving maids of Aberdeen,
    When they go to the dancing,
The young men all admires the sport,
    They are so neat and handsome.
        Fal de ral lal de ral.

It is well kent their face they paint,
    They are so vain and idle;
To busk and dress more time they pass,
    Than they do on their Bible.
      Fal, etc.

With duffle cardinals of different hue
    And cloaks of finest scarlet,
Which worn are I do declare
    By many whore and harlot.
      Fal, etc.

Their qualities come show to me —
    You'll not know't by their cleeding;
Dear neighbour then, I'll tell you plain,
    You'll find it by their breeding,
      Fal, etc.

They curse and swear and domineer
    And scold like any randy;
Their morning drink I really think,
    Is whisky gin or brandy.
      Fal, etc.

And if they chance to prove with child
    Or lose their reputation,
They then set up a bawdy house —
    And that's their occupation.
      Fal, etc.

Such bawds and bullies then turn thieves:
    Observe the dismal story,
By hangie's hand their lives they end —
    And that's called gallows glory!
      Fal de ral lal de ral.

admires — regular Scots form for 3rd pers. plur., present tense; *kent* — known;
busk — get ready; *cardinals* — short cloaks with hoods; *randy* — obstreporous beggar;
cleeding — clothing; *hangie* — the hangman.

                                            THE BROADSIDE MODE

A Highland Lad my Love was Born

A Highland lad my love was born,
The Lalland laws he held in scorn;
But he still was faithfu' to his clan,
My gallant, braw John Highlandman.

Chorus
Sing hey my braw John Highlandman!
Sing ho my braw John Highlandman!
There's not a lad in a' the lan'
Was match for my John Highlandman.

With his philibeg an' tartan plaid,
An' guid claymore down by his side,
The ladies' hearts he did trepan,
My gallant, braw John Highlandman.
   Sing hey, etc.

We ranged a' from Tweed to Spey,
An' liv'd like lords an' ladies gay;
For a Lalland face he feared none,
My gallant, braw John Highlandman.
   Sing hey, etc.

They banish'd him beyond the sea.
But ere the bud was on the tree,
Adown my cheeks the pearls ran,
Embracing my John Highlandman.
   Sing hey, etc.

But, och! they catch'd him at the last,
And bound him in a dungeon fast:
My curse upon them every one,
They've hang'd my braw John Highlandman!
   Sing hey, etc.

And now a widow, I must mourn
The pleasures that will ne'er return:
No comfort but a hearty can,
When I think on John Highlandman.
   Sing hey, etc.

                                        Robert Burns

philibeg — kilt; *Lalland* — lowland; *trepan* — capture.

THE BROADSIDE MODE   25

Farewell, ye dungeons dark and strong,
  The wretch's destinie!
M'Pherson's time will not be long
  On yonder gallows-tree.

        Chorus
  Sae rantingly, sae wantonly,
    Sae dauntingly gaed he:
  He play'd a spring, and danc'd it round,
    Below the gallows-tree.

O what is death but parting breath?
  On many a bloody plain
I've dar'd his face, and in this place
  I scorn him yet again!
    Sae rantingly, etc.

Untie these bands from off my hands,
  And bring to me my sword;
And there's no a man in all Scotland,
  But I'll brave him at a word.
    Sae rantingly, etc.

I've liv'd a life of sturt and strife;
  I die by treacherie:
It burns my heart I must depart,
  And not avengèd be.
    Sae rantingly, etc.

Now farewell light, thou sunshine bright,
  And all beneath the sky!
May coward shame distain his name,
  The wretch that dares not die!
    Sae rantingly, etc.

                            Robert Burns

spring — lively tune; *sturt* — trouble.

23   Solomon Corrected

The wisest king in days of yore,
   And best of prophets too,
Has signified in ancient lore,
   What mortal man should do:
And I presume you think that he
Knew what was what as well as we.
   With a fa, la, la, la, la, la, la.

And yet this man of mighty skill,
   Or sacred or profane
Was teased with an unbounded will
   Which made him still complain;
He prayed, he preached, he loved, he quaffed,
But seldom practised what he taught.
   With a fa, la, etc.

His house was so laid o'er with gold,
   That silver scarce was seen,
Yet wàs this monarch, we are told,
   Oft troubled with the spleen:
Had we been with his treasure crowned,
No dumps about us had been found.
   With a fa, la, etc.

The Fair, obedient to his laws,
   Before his sceptre fall,
Yet with chagrin he pined, because
   He could not serve them all:
But you and I had thought it best
To serve a few, and leave the rest.
   With a fa, la, etc.

With vast expense and princely care
   He raised a sumptuous pile,
On downy bed and velvet chair
   His sorrows to beguile;
But he had fetched a nap as sound
On a straw-bed upon the ground
   With a fa, la, etc.

He then endeav'ring to be gay,
    Rolled in a coach and eight,
By which he hoped to drive away
    From his uneasy thought;
He might as well, without his wheels,
Tripped it like us upon his heels.
    With a fa, la, etc.

At length he found the generous bowl,
    Replete with sprightly wine,
By intervals solaced his soul
    With cheerfulness divine:
And on that score the sage and we
To take a chirping cup agree.
    With a fa, la, etc.

Inspired with a devotion fit,
    A lofty dome he reared,
With costly gems he garnished it,
    To be the better heard;
But we're as well received who pray
From our low cells of mud and clay.
    With a fa, la, etc.

At last, since nought away could rub
    The causes of his pain,
He raised him in his royal tub,
    And preached that all was vain:
Since there's no help for vanity,
We'll drink, and be as vain as he.
    With a fa, la, etc.

Perhaps we've sung more than our share,
    Grown like our liquor stout,
Nor king nor prophet will we spare,
    For truth at last will out:
He needs not brag of Wisdom's rules,
Who can be taught by us two fools.
    With a fa, la, etc.

Alexander Robertson of Struan

BACCHANALIAN

or... or — either... or; *spleen* — ill-humour; *dumps* — depression; *pile* — large building; *chirping* — cheering; *devotion fit* — i.e. fit of devotion; *tub* — contemptuous term for a pulpit (esp. of puritan or nonconformist).

24   Todlen Hame

When I've a saxpence under my thumb,
Then I'll get credit in ilka toun:
But aye when I'm poor they bid me gang by;
O! poverty parts good company.
    Todlen hame, and todlen hame,
    Couldna my love come todlen hame?

Fair fa' the goodwife and send her good sale,
She gies us white bannocks to drink her ale;
Syne, if that her tippony chance to be sma',
We tak a good scour o't, and ca't awa'.
    Todlen hame, todlen hame,
    As round as a neep come todlen hame.

My kimmer and I lay down to sleep,
And twa pint-stoups at our bed's feet;
And aye when we waken'd we drank them dry:
What think ye of my wee kimmer and I?
    Todlen but, and todlen ben,
    Sae round as my loove comes todlen hame.

Leez me on liquor, my todlen dow,
Ye're aye sae good-humour'd when weeting your mou;
When sober sae sour, ye'll fight with a flee,
That 'tis a blyth sight to the bairns and me,
    When todlen hame, todlen hame,
    When round as a neep ye come todlen hame.

hame — home; *ilka* — each; *aye* — always; *gang* — go; *na* — not; *fa* — befall; *goodwife* — hostess; *syne* — then; *tippony* — twopenny ale; *sma'* — small (i.e. weak); *scour* — draught; *ca'* — drive; *neep* — turnip; *kimmer* — gossip; *stoup* — deep, narrow pitcher; *but... ben* — into both rooms of cottage; *round* — mellow; *loove* — indicating pronunciation still used by folksingers today; *leez...on* — hurrah for!; *dow* — dove; *weeting* — wetting; *mou* — mouth; *flee* — fly; *bairns* — children.

There were four drunken maidens
   Together did convene,
From twelve o'clock in a May morning
   Till ten rang out at e'en.
   Till ten rang out at e'en,
   And then they gi'ed it ower.
And there's four drunken maidens
   Down i' the Nether Bow.

When in came Nelly Paterson,
   With her fine satin gown:
Come sit about, ye maidens,
   And give to me some room,
   And give to me some room,
   Before that we gie't ower.
And there's four drunken maidens
   Down i' the Nether Bow.

When peacock and pigeon,
   And hedgehog and hare,
And all sorts of fine venison,
   Was well made ready there,
   And set before the maidens
   Before they gie'd it ower.
And there's four drunken maidens
   Down i' the Nether Bow.

e'en − evening; *gi'ed* − gave; *ower* − over; *Nether Bow* − lit. the 'lower bend' of the High Street in Edinburgh, before it turned into the Canongate.

26   Cauld Kail in Aberdeen

There's cauld kail in Aberdeen,
And castocks in Strabogie
Where ilka lad maun hae his lass
Then fie, gie me my cogie.

My cogie, Sirs, my cogie, Sirs,
    I canna want my cogie;
I wadna gie my three-girred cap
    For e'er a quine on Bogie.

There's Johnie Smith has got a wife
That scrimps him o' his cogie,
If she were mine, upon my life
I wad douk her in a bogie.
    My cogie, Sirs, etc.

Twa-three toddlin weans they hae,
The pride o' a' Strabogie;
When'er the totums cry for meat
She curses ay his cogie.
    O wae betide the three-girred cog!
        O wae betide the cogie,
    It does mair skaith than a' the ills
        That happen in Strabogie.

She fand him ance at Willie Sharp's,
And what they maist did laugh at,
She brak the bicker, spilt the drink,
And tightly gowffed his haffet.
    O wae betide, etc.

Yet here's to ilka honest chiel
Wha drinks wi' me a cogie,
As for ilk silly whingin fool
We'll drink him in a bogie.
    For I maun hae my cogie, sirs,
        I canna want my cogie;
    I wadna gie my three-girred cog
        For a' the quines in Bogie.

---

cauld — cold; *kail* — broth made of colewort; *castocks* — colewort stalks;
Stra(th)bogie — district in N.W. Aberdeenshire; *ilka* — each; *maun* — must; *cogie* —
wooden drinking cup girdled with metal bands; *na* — not; *want* — lack; *three-girred
cap* — cup with three bands; *quine* — wench; *scrimp* — deprive; *douk* — duck; *bogie* —
marsh; *weans* — children; *totums* — infants; *skaith* — harm; *Willie Sharp* — innkeeper's
name; *bicker* — wooden drinking vessel with one or two staves extended to form lugs;
tightly — soundly; *gowffed* — slapped; *baffet* — temple; *chiel* — fellow; *whingin* —
whining.

BACCHANALIAN   31

Hollo! keep it up, boys — and push round the glass,
Let each seize his bumper, and drink to his lass:
Away with dull thinking — tis madness to think —
And let those be sober who've nothing to drink.
   Tal de ral, etc.

Silence that vile clock, with its iron-tongu'd bell,
Of the hour that's departed still ringing the knell:
But what is't to us that the hours fly away?
'Tis only a signal to moisten the clay.
   Tal de ral, etc.

Huzza, boys! let each take a bumper in hand,
And stand — if there's any one able to stand.
How all things dance round me! — 'tis life, tho' my boys:
Of drinking and spewing how great are the joys!
   Tal de ral, etc.

My head! oh, my head! — but no matter, 'tis life;
Far better than moping at home with one's wife.
The pleasure of drinking you're sure must be grand,
When I'm neither able to think, speak, nor stand.
   Tal de ral, etc.

                                        Robert Fergusson

28   A Mournful Ditty from the Knight of Complaints
     What should I do up town? My business lies all in the Canongate! (Motto)

How blyth was I ilk day to see
     Auchleck come tripping doun
His ain forestairs at Netherbow
     To drink his dram at Noon!

          Chorus
Oh, the shades, the caller caller shades,
     Where I have oft complain'd

Till Luckie's bottle C.F.D.
   Was to the bottom drain'd!

I neither wanted drink nor dram
   Whan Tam Dick's house was nigh —
But now in Canongate I dwell,
   A dismal place and dry.
Oh, the shades, etc.

Hard fate that I should banish'd be,
   Gang heavily and mourn
Because I lo'ed the warmest dram
   That e'er in mouth did burn!
Oh, the shades, etc.

She brought a gill sae strong and sweet,
   The Knights stood drouthy by;
Even Pitcher Hume in dumbness gaz'd
   He was so very dry.
Oh, the shades, etc.

Our bottle and the little stoup
   That held our wee soup dram . . .
Ye thirsty Knights for liquor coup —
   I will not care a damn!
Oh, the shades, etc.

Adieu ye cooling shades, adieu;
   Fareweel my forenoon's gill;
By Tam Dick's fire I'll sit no more,
   My Horrors all to kill!
Oh, the shades, etc.

Robert Fergusson

A Mournful Ditty — was written for the Cape, a drinking club to which Fergusson belonged; *Knight of Complaints* — the Cape Club title of a certain Alexander Clapperton, in whose character the song is written; *Auchleck* — Gilbert Auchleck, cutler of Netherbow, in Edinburgh, whose Cape Club title was Sir Launce; *Netherbow* — continuation of High Street towards the Canongate; *caller* — cool; *Luckie* — the hostess; *C.F.D.* — abbreviation of the Cape Club's motto, 'Concordia Fratrium Decus' (harmony is the virtue of brothers); *Tam Dick* — tavern owner, not positively identified; *drouthy* — thirsty; *Pitcher* — Toastmaster; *wee soup* — small amount; *coup* — cup; *Horrors* — withdrawal symptoms.

My wife's a wanton, wee thing,
My wife's a wanton, wee thing,
My wife's a wanton, wee thing,
    She winna be guided by me.

She play'd the loon or she was married,
She play'd the loon or she was married,
She play'd the loon or she was married,
    She'll do it again or she die.

She sell'd her coat and she drank it,
She sell'd her coat and she drank it,
She row'd hersell in a blanket,
    She winna be guided for me.

She mind't na when I forbade her,
She mind't na when I forbade her,
I took a rung and I claw'd her,
    And a braw gude bairn was she.

Robert Burns

winna – won't; *play'd the loon* – kicked over the traces; *or* – before; *row'd* – rolled; *rung* – cudgel; *claw'd* – beat; *braw* – fine; *bairn* – child.

30   Rattlin, Roarin Willie

O, rattlin, roarin Willie,
    O, he held to the fair,
An' for to sell his fiddle
    And buy some other ware;
But parting wi' his fiddle,
    The saut tear blin't his e'e –
And, rattlin, roarin Willie
    Ye're welcome hame to me!

'O Willie, come sell your fiddle,
    O, sell your fiddle sae fine!
O Willie, come sell your fiddle,
    And buy a pint o' wine!'
'If I should sell my fiddle,
    The warld would think I was mad;
For mony a rantin day
    My fiddle and I hae had.'

As I cam by Crochallan,
    I cannily keekit ben;
Rattlin, roarin Willie
    Was sittin at yon boord-en';
Sittin at yon boord-en',
    And amang guid companie;
Rattlin, roarin Willie,
    Ye're welcome hame to me!

Robert Burns

rattlin — lively; *held to* — went towards; *saut* — salt; *rantin* — riotous; *Crochallan* — meeting place of the Crochallan Corps, 'a club of wits who took that title at the time of the raising of the fencible regiments' (Burns); *cannily* — cautiously; *keekit* — looked; *ben* — inwards; *Willie* (in st. 3) — William Dunbar, W.S., 'colonel of the Crochallan Corps'; *boord-en'* — table end.

31   John Barleycorn

There was three kings into the east,
    Three kings both great and high,
And they hae sworn a solemn oath
    John Barleycorn should die.

They took a plough and plough'd him down,
    Put clods upon his head,
And they hae sworn a solemn oath
    John Barleycorn was dead.

But the cheerful Spring came kindly on,
    And show'rs began to fall;
John Barleycorn got up again,
    And sore surpris'd them all.

The sultry suns of Summer came,
    And he grew thick and strong,
His head weel arm'd wi' pointed spears,
    That no one should him wrong.

The sober Autumn enter'd mild,
    When he grew wan and pale;
His bending joints and drooping head
    Show'd he began to fail.

His colour sicken'd more and more,
    He faded into age;
And then his enemies began
    To show their deadly rage.

They've taen a weapon, long and sharp,
    And cut him by the knee;
Then tied him fast upon a cart,
    Like a rogue for forgerie.

They laid him down upon his back,
    And cudgell'd him full sore;
They hung him up before the storm,
    And turn'd him o'er and o'er.

They filled up a darksome pit
    With water to the brim;
They heaved in John Barleycorn,
    There let him sink or swim.

They laid him out upon the floor,
    To work him further woe;
And still, as signs of life appear'd,
    They toss'd him to and fro.

They wasted, o'er a scorching flame,
    The marrow of his bones;
But a miller us'd him worst of all,
    For he crush'd him between two stones.

And they hae taen his very heart's blood,
    And drank it round and round;
And still the more and more they drank,
    Their joy did more abound.

John Barleycorn was a hero bold,
   Of noble enterprise,
For if you do but taste his blood,
   'Twill make your courage rise.

'Twill make a man forget his woe;
   'Twill heighten all his joy:
'Twill make the widow's heart to sing,
   Tho' the tear were in her eye.

Then let us toast John Barleycorn,
   Each man a glass in hand;
And may his great posterity,
   Ne'er fail in old Scotland!

Robert Burns

32 ·   Lady Onlie, honest Lucky

A' the lads o' Thorniebank,
   When they gae to the shore o' Bucky,
They'll step in an' tak a pint
   Wi' Lady Onlie, honest lucky.

            Chorus
Lady Onlie, honest Lucky,
   Brews gude ale at shore o' Bucky;
I wish her sale for her gude ale,
   The best on a' the shore o' Bucky.

Her house sae bien, her curch sae clean,
   I wat she is a dainty chuckie;
And cheery blinks the ingle-gleede
   O' Lady Onlie, honest lucky.
Lady Onlie, etc.

Robert Burns

a' – all; *gae* – go; *Bucky* – Buckie, fishing port in Banffshire; *Lucky* – hostess; *bien*
– comfortable; *curch* – kerchief; *chuckie* – sweetheart, dear; *ingle-gleede* – glowing
fire.

O Willie brew'd a peck o' maut,
   And Rob and Allan cam to see;
Three blyther hearts, that lee-lang night,
   Ye wad na found in Christendie.

Chorus
We are na fou, we're nae that fou,
   But just a drappie in our e'e;
The cock may craw, the day may daw,
   And ay we'll taste the barley bree.

Here are we met, three merry boys,
   Three merry boys I trow are we;
And mony a night we've merry been,
   And mony mae we hope to be!
We are na fou, etc.

It is the moon, I ken her horn,
   That's blinkin in the lift sae hie;
She shines sae bright to wyle us hame,
   But, by my sooth, she'll wait a wee!
We are na fou, etc.

Wha first shall rise to gang awa,
   A cuckold, coward loun is he!
Wha first beside his chair shall fa',
   He is the King amang us three!
We are na fou, etc.

Robert Burns

maut – malt; *blyther* – happier; *lee-lang* – live-long; *wad na* – would not have; *fou* – drunk; *drappie* – droplet; *e'e* – eye; *craw* – crow; *daw* – dawn; *ay* – still; *bree* – brew; *mae* – more; *blinkin* – shining; *lift* – sky; *hie* – high; *wyle* – entice; *sooth* – truth; *gang* – go; *loun* – rogue.

34   Hey ca' thro'

Here's to the dance of Dysart
And the kimmers of Largo
And the brides of Buckhaven
And the gossips of Leven.

> *Chorus*
> *Hey ca' thro' ca' thro',*
>   *For we have muckle to do;*
> *And hey ca' thro' ca' thro'*
>   *For we have muckle to do.*

And Johnnie Geordie rose
And he put on his clothes;
When he bang'd up his trumps
The lasses came in by the lumps.
And hey etc.

And they had muches and rails
And aprons wi' peacock tails
And a' sic busks sae bonnie –
Come dance wi our son Johnnie.
And hey etc.

Maggie she kiss'd the piper,
There could naebody wyte her;
She had nae siller I trow,
But she gae kisses anow.
And hey etc.

We have sheets to shape,
And we have beds to make,
And we have corn to shear,
And we have bairns to bear.
And hey etc.

ca' thro' – get work done; *Dysart, Largo, Buckhaven, Leven* – fishing villages in Fife;
kimmers – gossips; *muckle* – much; *bang'd* – struck; *trumps* – musical instrument
(with equivocal sense); *muches* – caps; *rails* – neckerchiefs; *busks* – finery; *wyte* –
blame; *nae* – no; *trow* – believe; *gae* – gave; *anow* – enough; *bairns* – children.

O well may the boatie row,
   And better may she speed;
And lees me on the boatie row,
   That wins the bairns' breed.

The boatie rows, the boatie rows,
   The boatie rows indeed,
And happy be the lot o' a'
   What wishes her to speed.

I cust my line in Largo bay,
   And fishes catch'd nine,
There was three to boil and three to fry,
   And three to bate the line.
O well may etc.

lees me on — blessings on; *bairns'* — children's; *a'* — all; *cust* — cast.

36   Ca' the Ewes

Ca' the ewes to the knows,
Ca' them where the heather grow,
Ca' them up and upper mair,
My bonny dearie.

Ye's get a maid baith stout and stark
To milk yere kye and work your wark,
And I will kiss you i' the dark —
My bonny dearie
Ca' the ewes etc.

Dear kind sir ye're sair to blame;
Ye mak me think a deal o' shame.
Your flattering words I do disdain,
I dinnae like to hear ye.
Ca' the ewes etc.

ca' — drive; *knows* — knolls; *upper mair* — higher up; *ye's* — you shall; *stark* — strong;
kye — cows; *sair* — sore; *dinnae* — do not.

My yellow-mou'd mistress, I bid you adieu,
For I've been too long in slavery with you,
With washing and scouring I'm seldom in bedy
And now I will go with my sodger laddie,
   My sodger laddie, my sodger laddie,
   The kisses are sweet of a sodger laddie.

With the crust of your loaf, and the dregs of your tea,
You fed your lap doggie far better than me,
With rinning and spinning, my head was unsteady,
But now I will go with my sodger laddie,
   My sodger laddie, etc.

For yarn, for yarn, you always did cry,
And look'd to my pirn, ay as ye went by;
Now the drums they do beat, and my bundle is ready,
And I'll go along with my sodger laddie,
   My sodger laddie, etc.

As women with men are always for use,
For washing and dressing, or plucking a goose;
Or drawing a chicken to make his diet ready,
O happy I'll be with my sodger laddie,
   My sodger laddie, etc.

A soldier that's married, I always do see,
Has always most money, if so they agree,
He calls her his honey, his dear and his lady,
Then I will go with my sodger laddie.
   My sodger laddie, etc.

If my fortune be bad, the truth I will tell,
It was through a bad mistress that so it befell;
If she sent me an errand, she cry'd, ay, where stay'd ye,
For which I will go with my sodger laddie.
   My sodger laddie, etc.

I went to the well, and lost a burn stoup,
And when I came home, she kicked my doup;
O was not this hard, by such a fine lady,
For which I will go with my sodger laddie.
   My sodger laddie, etc.

I'll always be ready, with needle and soap,
For possing and patching to serve the whole troop,
I'll be loving and kind, and live like a lady,
When I go abroad with my sodger laddie.
  My sodger laddie, etc.

In heat of battles, I'll keep on the flank,
With a stone in a stocking, and give them a clank.
If he be knock'd down, though he be my daddy,
I'll bring all his clink to my sodger laddie.
  My sodger laddie, etc.

For robbing the dead is no theivish trick,
I'll rifle his breeches, and then his knapsack,
But yet on a friend I'll not be so ready,
If he's been acquaint with my sodger laddie,
  My sodger laddie, etc.

Then as rich as a Jew, I'll return yet I hope,
And ask my old lady if she's found her burn stoup,
And all my days after, I'll live like a lady,
On the gold I've got, with my sodger laddie,
  My sodger laddie, my sodger laddie,
  The kisses are sweet of a sodger laddie.

yellow-mou'd − yellow-mouthed (jaundiced); *sodger* − soldier; *pirn* − bobbin of a
spinning-wheel; *ay* − always; *burn* − well, stream; *stoup* − pitcher; *doup* − arse;
possing − washing clothes by lifting them from the tub and kneading them; *clink* −
money.

38   O Merry may the Maid be

O merry may the maid be
  That marries with the miller,
For foul day and fair day
  He's ay bringing till her;
Has ay a penny in his purse
  For dinner and for supper;
And gin he please, a good fat cheese,
  And lumps of yellow butter.

When Jamie first did woo me,
   I speir'd what was his calling;
'Fair maid,' says he, 'O come and see,
   Ye're welcome to my dwalling.'
Though I was shy, yet I cou'd spy
   The truth of what he told me,
And that his house was warm and couth,
   And room in it to hold me.

Behind the door a bag of meal,
   And in the kist was plenty
Of good hard cakes his mither bakes;
   And bannocks were na scanty.
A good fat sow, a sleeky cow
   Was standin in the byre,
Whilst lazy pouss with mealy mouse
   Was playing at the fire.

'Good signs are these,' my mither says,
   And bids me tak the miller;
For foul day and fair day
   He's ay bringing till her;
For meal and malt she does na want,
   Nor ony thing that's dainty;
And now and then a keckling hen
   To lay her eggs in plenty

In winter when the wind and rain
   Blaws o'er the house and byre,
He sits beside a clean hearth stane
   Before a rousing fire;
With nut-brown ale he tells his tale,
   Which rows him o'er fou nappy –
Who'd be a king, a petty thing,
   When a miller lives so happy?

Sir John Clerk

O Merry may the Maid be – the first stanza is traditional.

ay – always; *till* – to; *gin* – if; *speir'd* – asked; *couth* – comfortable; *kist* – chest;
bannock – thick cake of barley or pease meal; *na* – not; *bringing* – fetching money;
keckling – cackling; *rows* – rolls; *fou nappy* – drunk with ale.

O the dusty miller, O the dusty miller,
Dusty was his coat, dusty was his colour,
Dusty was the kiss I got frae the miller!
O the dusty miller with the dusty coat,
He will spend a shilling ere he win a groat!

frae – from; *groat* – small coin.

40   The Ploughman

The ploughman he's a bonnie lad,
    His mind is ever true, jo;
His garters knit below the knee,
    His bonnet it is blue, jo.

> *Chorus*
> *Sing up wi't a', the ploughman lad,*
> *And hey the merry ploughman;*
> *O' a' the trades that I do ken,*
> *Commend me to the ploughman.*

As wakin' forth upon a day,
    I met a jolly ploughman,
I tald him I had lands to plough,
    If he wad prove true, man.
Sing up wi't a', etc.

He says, 'My dear, tak ye nae fear,
    I'll fit you till a hair, jo;
I'll cleave it up, and hit it down.
    And water-furrow't fair, jo.
Sing up wi't a', etc.

I hae three ousen in my plough,
    Three better ne'er plough'd ground, jo.
The foremost ox is lang and sma',
    The twa are plump and round, jo.'
Sing up wi't a', etc.

Then he wi' speed did yoke his plough,
    Which be a gaud was driven, jo!
But when he wan between the stilts,
    I thought I was in heaven, jo!
Sing up wi't a', etc.

But the foremost ox fell in the fur,
    The tither twa did founder;
The ploughman lad he breathless grew,
    In faith it was nae wonder.
Sing up wi't a', etc.

But a sykie risk, below the hill,
    The plough she took a stane, jo,
Which gart the fire flee frae the sock,
    The ploughman gied a grane, jo.
Sing up wi't a', etc.

I hae plough'd east, I hae plough'd west,
    In weather foul and fair, jo;
But the sairest ploughing e'er I plough'd,
    Was ploughing amang hair, jo.
        Sing up wi't a', and in wi't a',
        And hey my merry ploughman;
        O' a' the trades, and crafts I ken,
        Commend me to the ploughman.

jo — sweetheart; *wi't a'* — with it all (i.e. with the penis); *till* — to; *water-furrow* — make a deep furrow to conduct water from the land; *hae* — have; *ousen* — oxen; *lang* — long; *sma'* — slender; *gaud* — goad; *stilts* — handles of the plough; *fur* — ditch, furrow; *tither* — other; *sykie* — wet; *risk* —noise made when plough cuts through roots; *stane* — stone; *flee* — fly; *gied* — gave; *grane*— groan; *sairest* — sorest.

41   O can ye labour Lee

I fee'd a man at Martinmas,
    Wi arle pennies three;
But a' the fau't I had to him,
    He coudna labour lee.

'O can ye labour lee, young man,
    O can ye labour lee?
Gae back the road ye cam agin,
    Ye shall never scorn me.

A stibble rig is easy plough'd,
    An' fallow land is free;
But what a silly coof is he,
    That canna labour lee.'

The spretty bush, an' benty knowe,
    The ploughman points his sock in,
He sheds the roughness, lays it by,
    An' baudly ploughs his yokin'.

arle pennies – payment made in token of employment; *labour* – plough; *lee* – pasture (fig., woman's sexual organs); *fau't* – fault; *stibble rig* – stubble field (fig., woman's sexual organs); *coof* – fool; *spretty* – rushy; *benty knowe* – hill covered with bent grass; *sheds* – parts; *by* – aside; *bauldly* – boldly; *yokin* – the time oxen or horses are in harness, vigorous effort.

42   The Mucking o' Geordie's Byre

The mucking of Geordie's byre,
    And shooling the grupe sae clean,
Has gard me weit my cheiks
    And greit with baith my een.
        It was ne'er my father's will,
            Nor yet my mother's desire,
        That e'er I should file my fingers,
            Wi' mucking of Geordie's byre.

The mouse is a merry beast,
    And the moudewort wants the e'en:
But the warld shall ne'er get wit
    Sae merry as we ha'e been.
        It was ne'er, etc.

mucking – cleaning out; *shooling* – shovelling; *grupe* – hollow behind stalls of horses or cattle for receiving dung and urine; *sae* – so; *gard* – made; *weit* – wet; *greit* – weep; *een* – eyes; *file* – dirty; *moudewort* – mole; *e'en* – eyes; *wit* – knowledge.

The auld man's mear's dead;
　The puir body's mear's dead;
　　A mile aboon Dundee.

There was hay to ca', and lint to lead,
A hunder hotts o' muck to spread,
And peats and truffs and a' to lead —
　And yet the jaud to dee!

She had the fiercie and the fleuk,
The wheozloch and the wanton yeuk;
On ilka knee she had a breuk —
　What ail'd the beast to dee?

She was lang-tooth'd and blench-lippit,
Heam-hough'd and haggis-fittit,
Lang-neckit, chandler-chaftit,
　And yet the jaud to dee!

> ? Patrick Birnie (fl. 1710)

auld — old; *mear* — mare; *puir* — poor; *aboon* — above; *ca'* — fetch; *lint* — flax; *hunder* — hundred; *hotts* — heaps, loads; *muck* — dung; *truffs* — turfs; *jaud* — jade; *fiercie* — violent hysteria; *fleuk* — diarrhoea; *wheezloch* — short-windedness; *wanton* — girth by which dung-baskets were fastened; *yeuk* — itch; *ilka* — each; *breuk* — boil; *blench-lippit* — white-mouthed; *heam-hough'd* — with upper legs shaped like the curved pieces of metal fixed over a draught horse's collar; *haggis-fittit* — with haggis-shaped hooves; *chandler-chaftit* — with jaws like candlesticks (i.e. thin).

44　　　Man was made to Mourn

When chill November's surly blast
　Made fields and forests bare,
One ev'ning, as I wander'd forth
　Along the banks of Ayr,
I spied a man, whose aged step
　Seem'd weary, worn with care;
His face was furrow'd o'er with years,
　And hoary was his hair.

'Young stranger, whither wand'rest thou?'
  Began the rev'rend Sage;
'Does thirst of wealth thy step constrain,
  Or youthful Pleasure's rage?
Or haply, prest with cares and woes,
  Too soon thou hast began
To wander forth, with me to mourn
  The miseries of Man.

The sun that overhangs yon moors,
  Out-spreading far and wide,
Where hundreds labour to support
  A haughty lordling's pride; —
I've seen yon weary winter-sun
  Twice forty times return;
And ev'ry time has added proofs,
  That Man was made to mourn.

O Man! while in thy early years,.
  How prodigal of time!
Mis-spending all thy precious hours —
  Thy glorious, youthful prime!
Alternate Follies take the sway;
  Licentious Passions burn;
Which tenfold force gives Nature's law,
  That Man was made to mourn.

Look not alone on youthful Prime,
  Or Manhood's active might;
Man then is useful to his kind,
  Supported is his right:
But see him on the edge of life,
  With Cares and Sorrows worn;
Then Age and Want — oh! ill-match'd pair —
  Show Man was made to mourn.

A few seem favourites of Fate,
  In Pleasure's lap carest;
Yet, think not all the Rich and Great
  Are likewise truly blest:
But oh! what crouds in ev'ry land,
  All the wretched and forlorn,
Thro' weary life this lesson learn,
  That Man was made to mourn!

Many and sharp the num'rous Ills
   Inwoven with our frame!
More pointed still we make ourselves
   Regret, Remorse, and Shame!
And Man, whose heav'n erected face
   The smiles of love adorn, —
Man's inhumanity to Man
   Makes countless thousands mourn!

See yonder poor, o'erlabour'd wight, ,
   So abject, mean, and vile,
Who begs a brother of the earth
   To give him leave to toil;
And see his lordly *fellow-worm,*
   The poor petition spurn,
Unmindful, though a weeping wife
   And helpless offspring mourn.

If I'm design'd yon lordling's slave,
   By Nature's law design'd,
Why was an independent wish
   E'er planted in my mind?
If not, why am I subject to
   His cruelty, or scorn?
Or why has Man the will and pow'r
   To make his fellow mourn?

Yet, let not this too much, my Son,
   Disturb thy youthful breast:
This partial view of human-kind
   Is surely not the *last!*
The poor, oppressèd, honest man
   Had never, sure, been born,
Had there not been some recompense
   To comfort those that mourn!

O Death! the poor man's dearest friend,
   The kindest and the best!
Welcome the hour my aged limbs
   Are laid with thee at rest!
The Great, the Wealthy fear thy blow,
   From pomp and pleasure torn;
But, Oh! a blest relief to those
   That weary-laden mourn!'

                               Robert Burns

45   Belial's Sons

Belial's sons,
Who with your tones
And your groans
    Cheate the people.

And lyk a mouse,
Still the pouse
Of every house
    That hes a steeple.

Damned sprites,
Lyk hypocrites,
On the streets
    Disappointed . . .

Ill wishers,
Stipend fishers,
Kirk pishers
    At the wall.

Whig beasties,
Sathones questies,
From your nesties
    Soon be your fall.

Back byters,
Pulpit flyters,
Kirk shyters
    At the altar.

The deil send you,
But God mend you,
Or else end you
    In a halter.

Belial's Sons – this song reflects the Episcopalian and Jacobite outlook in the 1690s; *pouse* – pulse; *Sathon* – Satan; *questies* – ? birds of prey; *flyters* – mudslingers; *deil* – devil.

To daunton me, to daunton me,
Do you ken the thing that would daunton me?
Eighty-eight, and eighty-nine,
And a' the dreary years since syne,
With Sess and Press, and Presbytry,
Good Faith, this had liken till a daunton me.

But to wanton me, but to wanton me,
Do you ken the thing that would wanton me?
To see gude corn upon the rigs,
And banishment to a' the Whigs,
And Right restor'd where Right should be,
O! these are the things would wanton me!

But to wanton me, but to wanton me,
And ken ye what maist would wanton me?
To see King James at Edinburgh Cross,
With fifty thousand foot and horse,
And the Usurper forc'd to flee —
O this is what maist would wanton me!

daunton — daunt; *ken* — know; *eighty-eight, and eighty-nine* — the exile of James VII
and coming of William of Orange in 1688-9; *syne* — then; *Sess* — cess (tax); *Press* —
impressing of men for service in army or navy; *had liken till* — would have been most
likely to; *wanton* — pleasure; *rigs* — ridges; *maist* — most.

47   The Tears of Scotland

Mourn, hapless Caledonia, mourn
Thy banish'd peace, thy laurels torn!
Thy sons, for valour long renown'd,
Lie slaughter'd on their native ground;
Thy hospitable roofs no more
Invite the stranger to the door;
In smoky ruins sunk they lie,
The monuments of cruelty.

The wretched owner sees, afar,
His all become the prey of war;
Bethinks him of his babes and wife,
Then smites his breast, and curses life.

Thy swains are famish'd on the rocks,
Where once they fed their wanton flocks:
Thy ravish'd virgins shriek in vain;
Thy infants perish on the plain.

What boots it, then, in ev'ry clime,
Thro' the wide-spreading waste of time,
Thy martial glory, crown'd with praise,
Still shone with undiminish'd blaze?
Thy tow'ring spirit now is broke,
Thy neck is bended to the yoke:
What foreign arms could never quell,
By civil rage and rancour fell.

The rural pipe and merry lay
No more shall cheer the happy day:
No social scenes of gay delight
Beguile the dreary winter night:
No strains, but those of sorrow, flow,
And nought be heard but sounds of woe,
While the pale phantoms of the slain
Glide nightly o'er the silent plain.

O baneful cause, oh, fatal morn,
Accurs'd to ages yet unborn!
The sons against their fathers stood;
The parent shed his children's blood.
Yet, when the rage of battle ceas'd,
The victor's soul was not appeas'd:
The naked and forlorn must feel
Devouring flames, and murd'ring steel!

The pious mother doom'd to death,
Forsaken, wanders o'er the heath,
The bleak wind whistles round her head,
Her helpless orphans cry for bread,
Bereft of shelter, food, and friend,
She views the shades of night descend,
And, stretch'd beneath th' inclement skies,
Weeps o'er her tender babes, and dies.

Whilst the warm blood bedews my veins,
And unimpair'd remembrance reigns,
Resentment of my country's fate
Within my filial breast shall beat;
And, spite of her insulting foe,
My sympathizing verse shall flow,
'Mourn, hapless Caledonia, mourn
Thy banish'd peace, thy laurels torn.'

                                        Tobias Smollett

The Tears of Scotland — written in 1746, after the battle of Culloden.

48   It was a' for our rightfu' King

It was a' for our rightfu' King
    We left fair Scotland's strand;
It was a' for our rightfu' King
    We e'er saw Irish land, my dear,
    We e'er saw Irish land.

Now a' is done that men can do,
    And a' is done in vain;
My Love and Native Land fareweel,
    For I maun cross the main, my dear,
    For I maun cross the main.

He turn'd him right and round about,
    Upon the Irish shore;
And gae his bridle-reins a shake,
    With, Adieu for evermore, my dear,
    And adieu for evermore.

The soger frae the wars returns,
    The sailor frae the main,
But I hae parted frae my Love,
    Never to meet again, my dear,
    Never to meet again.

When day is gane, and night is come,
    And a' folk bound to sleep;
I think on him that's far awa,
    The lee-lang night and weep, my dear,
    The lee-lang night and weep.

Robert Burns

It was a' for our rightfu' King — set in the year of James VII's Irish campaigns; *a'* —
all; *maun* — must; *gae* — gave; *soger* — soldier; *lee-lang* — live-long.

49   The Pretender's Manifesto

Have you any laws to mend,
Or have you any grievance?
I am a Hero to my trade
And truly a most leal prince.
Would you have war, would you have peace,
Would you be free of taxes? —
Come chaping at my father's door,
You need not doubt of access!

Religion, Laws and Liberty
Ye ken are bonny words, sirs,
They shall be all made sure to you
If ye'll fight wi' your swords, sirs.
The nation's debt we soon shall pay
If ye'll support our right, boys;
No sooner we are brought in play
Than all things shall be tight, boys.

Ye ken that by an union base
Your ancient Kingdom's undone,
That all your ladies, lords and lairds
Gangs up and lives at London.
Nae longer that we will allow,
For crack —— it goes asunder,
What took sic time and pains to do;
And let the warld wonder!

I'm sure for seven years and mair
Ye've heard of sad oppression;
And this is all the good ye got
O' the Hanover succession.
For absolute power and popery,
Ye ken its a' but nonsense;
I here swear to secure to you
Your Liberty of Conscience.

And for your mair encouragement
Ye shall be pardon'd byganes;
Nae mair fight on the continent
And leave behind your dry banes.
Then come away and dinnae stay —
What gars ye look sae lawndart?
I'd have ye run and not delay
To join my father's standard.

                                          Alison Cockburn

leal — loyal; *chaping* — knocking; *ken* — know; *tight* — tidy; *gangs* — goes; *nae* — no;
sic — such; *mair* — more; *byganes* — bygones; *banes*   — bones; *dinnae* — don't; *gars*
— makes; *sae* — so; *lawndart* — doltish.

50   You're welcome, Charlie Stewart

You're welcome Charlie Stewart,
You're welcome Charlie Stewart,
You're welcome Charlie Stewart,
There's none so right as thou art . . .

Hadst thou Culloden Battle won,
Poor Scotland had not been undone,
Nor butcher'd been, with sword and gun,
By Lockhart and such cowards.
    You're welcome, etc.

Kind Providence, to thee a friend,
A lovely maid did timely send,
To save thee from a fearful End,
Thou charming Charlie Stewart.
    You're welcome, etc.

When ere I take a glass of wine,
I drink confusion to the swine;
But health to him that will combine
To fight for Charlie Stewart.
You're welcome, etc.

The Ministry may Scotland maul,
But our brave Hearts they'll ne'er enthrall;
We'll fight, like Britons, one and all,
For Liberty and Stewart.
You're welcome, etc.

Then haste, ye Britons, and set on
Your lawful King upon the Throne;
To Hanover we'll drive each one,
Who will not fight for Stewart.
You're welcome, etc.

Lockhart – a major of Cholmondley's Regiment and a lowland Scot, notorious for
his brutal treatment of Jacobite prisoners; *maid* – Flora MacDonald, who sheltered
Prince Charles after Culloden.

51   Tho' Geordie reigns in Jamie's stead

Tho' Geordie reigns in Jamie's stead,
I'm grieved yet scorn to shaw that,
I'll ne'er look down nor hang my head
On rebel Whig for a' that;
For still I trust that Providence
Will us relieve from a' that,
Our royal Prince is weel in Health,
And will be here for a' that.

> *Chorus*
> *For a' that, and a' that*
> *And thrice as muckle's a' that:*
> *He's far beyond the seas the night,*
> *Yet he'll be here for a' that.*

He's far beyond Dumblain the night,
Whom I love weel for a' that;
He wears a pistol by his side
That makes me blyth for a' that,

And tho' he's o'er the seas the night,
He'll soon be here for a' that.
    And a' that, etc.

He wears a broadsword by his side,
And weel he kens to draw that,
The target and the Highland plaid,
The shoulder-belt and a' that;
A bonnet bound with ribbons blue,
The white Cockade, and a' that,
And tho' beyond the seas the night,
Yet he'll be here for a' that.
    And a' that, etc.

The Whigs think a' that Weal is won,
But faith they ma'na fa' that;
They think our loyal hearts dung down,
But we'll be blyth for a' that.
    And a' that, etc.

But O what will the Whigs say syne,
When they're mista'en in a' that?
When Geordie mun fling by the Crown,
His hat and wig, and a' that?
The flames will get baith hat and wig,
As often they've done a' that;
Our Highland Lad will get the Crown,
And we'll be blyth for a' that.
    And a' that, etc.

O! then your bra' militia lads
Will be rewarded duly,
When they fling by their black Cockades,
A hellish colour truly.
As night is banish'd by the day,
The white shall drive awa that;
The Sun shall then his Beams display,
And we'll be blyth for a' that.
    And a' that, etc.

shaw – show; *a'* – all; *weel* – well; *muckle* – much; *the night* – tonight; *white* –
Jacobite colour; *weal* – realm; *ma'na fa'* – must not get; *dung down* – subdued; *syne*
– then; *mun* – must; *baith* – both; *bra'* – brave; *black* – Hanoverian colour.

O Brother Sandie, hear ye the news?
   Lillibulero, bullen a la.
An army's just coming without any shoes,
   Lillibulero, bullen a la.
   To arms, to arms, brave boys, to arms;
A true British cause for your courage doth ca';
   Court, country, and city, against a banditti,
   Lillibulero, bullen a la.

The Pope sends us over a bonny young lad, *etc.,*
Who, to court British favour, wears a Highland plaid, *etc.,*
   To arms, etc.

A Protestant Church from Rome doth advance, *etc.,*
And, what is more rare, brings freedom from France, *etc.,*
   To arms, etc.

If this shall surprise you, there's news stranger yet, *etc.,*
He brings Highland money to pay British debt, *etc.,*
   To arms, etc.

You must take it in coin which the country affords, *etc.,*
Instead of broad pieces, he pays with broad-swords, *etc.,*
   To arms, etc.

And sure this is paying you in the best ore,
   Lillibulero, bullen a la,
For who once is thus paid will never want more,
   Lillibulero, bullen a la.
   To arms, to arms, brave boys, to arms:
A true British cause for your courage doth ca';
   Court, country, and city, against a banditti,
   Lillibulero, bullen a la.

Sandie – Alexander; *ca'* – call; *Lillibulero, bullen a la* – refrain of militant Protestant song of late seventeenth century, here used in a Whig song against Prince Charles.

As I be ga'an up the street,
   I met a bra' man in te rear,
Who speer'd at me, wha's man I be
   And wha's cockade I wear.
'I wear the Royal Charlie's,
   And he's our lawful Prince;
And soon I hope to see him crown'd
   Without the help of France.

And gin ye'd no be angry,
   Ae question I wad speer,
And that is, fa's man ye be,
   And fa's cockade ye wear?'
'I wear the Royal Geordie's,
   And he's come frae Hanover,
For to support the covenant,
   The Whigs did bring him over.'

'It's a' for that same story,
   I wadna' think it much,
For to cut out baith your lugs,
   And put them in your pouch;
And then go tell Duke Willie,
   For he canno' speak Erse;
That highland-man's cut baith your lugs,
   And throw them in his face.'

ga'an — walking; bra' — brave; speer'd — asked; wha's — whose; cockade — party
badge or ribbon worn in hat; gin — if; ae — one; fa's — whose; a' — all; wadna' —
would not; baith — both; lugs — ears; Duke Willie — William, Duke of Cumberland;
Erse — Gaelic.

54   O wow, Marget, are ye in?

'O wow, Marget, are ye in?
I nae sooner heard it, but I boot to rin
Down the gate to tell ye, down the gate to tell ye,
Down the gate to tell ye: we'll no' be left our skin!

For o, dear woman, o dear! o dear!
The like o' this was never heard since Marr's year:
The French and the 'Mericains they will a' be here,
And we will a' be murdered, o dear, dear!

And o wow, woman, I doubt, I doubt,
They will bring in black popery a' round about,
And sad desolation, and sad desolation,
And sad desolation in a' the kirks about.

But well did I ken, that a' was nae right,
For I dream'd o' rad and green the whole last night,
And twa cats fighting, and twa cats fighting,
And twa cats fighting: I wakened wi' a fright.

But hae ye na mind in this very floor
How we rigg'd out ourselves for the Shiriffmoor,
Wi' stanes in our aprons, wi' stanes in our aprons,
Wi' stanes in our aprons: we did them skaith, I'm sure!

O bide a wee, Marget, I think I hear a gun' —
'Hout awa, woman, 'twas but me breaking wind!
I'm blyth whan it wins awa, blyth whan it wins awa,
Blyth whan it wins awa wi' sae little din.'

O farewell, woman, for I man go rin,
I wonder gif our neighbour Elspa be in,
And auld Raby Barber and auld Raby Barber,
And auld Raby Barber, and I man tell him!

O wow, Marget — dates from 1779 when Paul Jones and his small Franco-American
naval force captured seventeen ships off the British coast and made an unsuccessful
attempt to take the port of Leith; *boot* — simply had to; *gate* — way; *no'* — not;
Marr's year — 1715, when the Earl of Mar commanded the Highlanders against
Argyll; *a'* — all; *kirks* — churches; *ken* — know; *hae* — have; *Shiriffmoor* — Sheriffmuir
(battle), 1715; *stanes* — stones; *skaith* — damage; *bide a wee* — stay a little; *awa* —
away; *maun* — must; *gif* — if: *auld* — old.

55   The Hunting of the Wren

'Will ye go to the wood?' quo' Fozie Mozie,
'Will ye go to the wood?' quo' Johnie Rednozie,

'Will ye go to the wood?' quo' Foslin' ene,
'Will ye go to the wood?' quo' brither and kin.

'What to do there?' quo' Fozie Mozie,
'What to do there?' quo' Johnie Rednozie,
'What to do there?' quo' Foslin' ene,
'What to do there?' quo' brither and kin.

'To slay the wren,' quo' Fozie Mozie,
'To slay the wren,' quo' Johnie Rednozie,
'To slay the wren,' quo' Foslin' ene,
'To slay the wren,' quo' brither and kin.

'What way will we get her hame?' quo' Fozie Mozie,
'What way will we get her hame?' quo' Johnie Rednozie,
'What way will we get her hame?' quo' Foslin' ene,
'What way will we get her hame?' quo' brither and kin.

'We'l hyre carts and horse,' quo' Fozie Mozie,
'We'l hyre carts and horse,' quo' Johnie Rednozie,
'We'l hyre carts and horse,' quo' Foslin' ene,
We'l hyre carts and horse,' quo' brither and kin.

'What way will we get her in?' quo' Fozie Mozie,
'What way will we get her in?' quo' Johnie Rednozie,
'What way will we get her in?' quo' Foslin' ene,
'What way will we get her in?' quo' brither and kin.

'We'l drive down the door-cheeks,' quo' Fozie Mozie,
'We'l drive down the door-cheeks,' quo' Johnie Rednozie,
'We'l drive down the door-cheeks,' quo' Foslin' ene,
'We'l drive down the door-cheeks,' quo' brither and kin.

'I'll hae a wing,' quo' Fozie Mozie,
'I'll hae anither,' quo' Johnie Rednozie,
'I'll hae a leg,' quo' Foslin' ene,
'And I'll hae anither,' quo' brither and kin.

Wren — perhaps originally 'the body of a royal sacrifice, in this case the King of the Birds' . . . In performance 'memories of ancient defiance are preserved' (A.L. Lloyd); *ene* — eyes; *brither* — brother; *hame* — home.

Heard ye o' the tree o' France,
    I watna what's the name o't;
Around it a' the patriots dance,
    Weel Europe kens the fame o't.
It stands where ance the Bastille stood,
    A prison built by kings, man,
When Superstition's hellish brood
    Kept France in leading strings, man.

Upo' this tree there grows sic fruit,
    Its virtues a' can tell, man;
It raises man aboon the brute,
    Its maks him ken himsel, man.
Gif ance the peasant taste a bit,
    He's greater than a lord, man,
An' wi' the beggar shares a mite
    O' a' he can afford, man.

This fruit is worth a' Afric's wealth,
    To comfort us 'twas sent, man:
To gie the sweetest blush o' health,
    An' mak us a' content, man.
It clears the een, it cheers the heart,
    Maks high and low gude friends, man;
And he wha acts the traitor's part
    It to perdition sends, man.

My blessings aye attend the chiel
    Wha pitied Gallia's slaves, man,
And staw a branch, spite o' the deil,
    Frae yont the western waves, man.
Fair Virtue water'd it wi' care,
    And now she sees wi' pride, man,
How weel it buds and blossoms there,
    Its branches spreading wide, man.

But vicious folks aye hate to see
    The works o' Virtue thrive, man;
The courtly vermin's banned the tree,
    And grat to see it thrive, man;

King Loui' thought to cut it down,
    When it was unco sma', man;
For this the watchman cracked his crown,
    Cut aff his head and a', man.

A wicked crew syne, on a time,
    Did tak a solemn aith, man,
It ne'er should flourish to its prime,
    I wat they pledged their faith, man.
Awa' they gaed wi' mock parade,
    Like beagles hunting game, man,
But soon grew weary o' the trade
    And wished they'd been at hame, man.

For Freedom, standing by the tree,
    Her sons did loudly ca', man;
She sang a sang o' liberty,
    Which pleased them ane and a', man.
By her inspired, the new-born race
    Soon drew the avenging steel, man;
The hirelings ran — her foes gied chase,
    And banged the despot weel, man.

Let Britain boast her hardy oak,
    Her poplar and her pine, man,
Auld Britain ance could crack her joke,
    And o'er her neighbours shine, man.
But seek the forest round and round,
    And soon 'twill be agreed, man,
That sic a tree can not be found,
    'Twixt London and the Tweed, man.

Without this tree, alake this life
    Is but a vale o' woe, man;
A scene o' sorrow mixed wi' strife,
    Nae real joys we know, man.
We labour soon, we labour late,
    To feed the titled knave, man;
And a' the comfort we're to get
    Is that ayont the grave, man.

POLITICS

63

Wi' plenty o' sic trees, I trow,
  The warld would live in peace, man;
The sword would help to mak a plough,
  The din o' war wad cease, man.
Like brethren in a common cause,
  We'd on each other smile, man;
And equal rights and equal laws
  Wad gladden every isle, man.

Wae worth the loon wha wadna eat
  Sic halesome dainty cheer, man;
I'd gie my shoon frae aff my feet,
  To taste sic fruit, I swear, man.
Syne let us pray, auld England may
  Sure plant this far-famed tree, man;
And blythe we'll sing, and hail the day
  That gave us liberty, man.

attrib. Robert Burns

watna – don't know; *weel* – well; *ance* – once; *sic* – such; *a'* – all; *aboon* – above;
maks – makes; *ken* – know; *gif* – if; *e'en* – eyes; *aye* – always; *chiel* – man; *staw* –
stole; *deil* – devil; *yont* – beyond; *grat* – wept; *unco* – very; *syne* – then; *aith* –
oath; *wat* – am sure; *gaed* – went; *hame* – home; *ca'* – call; *auld* – old; *ayont* –
beyond; *wae worth* – woe to; *loon* – fellow.

57   As I stood by yon roofless Tower

As I stood by yon roofless tower,
  Where the wa'-flower scents the dewy air,
Where the houlet mourns in her ivy bower,
  And tells the midnight moon her care:

Chorus
A lassie all alone was making her moan,
  Lamenting our lads beyond the sea;
In the bluidy wars they fa', and our honour's gane and a',
  And broken-hearted we maun die.

The winds were laid, the air was still,
    The stars they shot alang the sky;
The tod was howling on the hill,
    And the distant-echoing glens reply.
The lassie, etc.

The burn, adown its hazelly path,
    Was rushing by the ruin'd wa',
Hasting to join the sweeping Nith
    Whase roarings seem'd to rise and fa'.
The lassie etc.

The cauld, blae north was streaming forth
    Her lights, wi' hissing, eerie din;
Athort the lift they start and shift,
    Like Fortune's favours, tint as win.
The lassie etc.

Now, looking over firth and fauld,
    Her horn the pale-fac'd Cynthia rear'd,
When, lo, in form of Minstrel auld,
    A stern and stalwart ghaist appear'd.
The lassie etc.

And frae his harp sic strains did flow,
    Might rous'd the slumbering Dead to hear;
But Oh, it was a tale of woe,
    As ever met a Briton's ear.
The lassie etc.

He sang wi' joy his former day,
    He weeping wail'd his latter times:
But what he said it was nae play,
    I winna ventur't in my rhymes.
The lassie etc.

Robert Burns

houlet – owl; *gane* – gone; *maun* – must; *tod* – fox; *burn* – brook; *Nith* – river in
Dumfriesshire; *blae* – livid; *athort* – athwart; *lift* – sky; *tint as win* – lost as soon as
won; *fauld* – fold; *auld* – old; *ghaist* – ghost; *might* – such as might have; *winna* –
will not.

58 The Terrors of God invading the Soul

O that the grief surrounding me,
  Were in a balance laid,
And my extreme calamity
  Were now against it weigh'd!

Then let an equal judge appear,
  His thoughts to signify,
Which scale the greatest weight does bear,
  He'd soon decide with me.

My crosses over-weigh my cries,
  My loads of woe and pain
Exceed the pond'rous sand that lies
  Around the ebbing main.

Unutterable are the groans,
  My weary soul oppress:
Nor have I words to speak my moans,
  Or shew my deep distress.

The arrows of th'almighty God
  Stick fast within my heart;
Each fest'ring wound burns up my blood,
  And gives me deadly smart.

Arrows, whose heads like flaming eyes,
  And pointed light'ning shine:
Steep'd in the strongest dregs and lees,
  Of fiery wrath divine.

The poison thereof raging high,
  Soon spreads without control;
Drinks up and drains my spirits dry,
  And eats into my soul.

God's threat'ning terrors all drawn out,
  In order and array,
For battle, closing me about,
  Invade me every way.

Ralph Erskine

O God of Bethel! by whose hand
    thy people still are fed;
Who through this weary pilgrimage
    hast all our fathers led.

Our vows, our pray'rs we now present
    before thy throne of grace;
God of our fathers! be the God
    of their succeeding race.

Through each perplexing path of life
    our wand'ring footsteps guide;
Give us each day our daily bread,
    and raiment fit provide.

O spread thy cov'ring wings around
    till all our wand'rings cease,
And at our Father's loved abode
    our souls arrive in peace.

Such blessings from thy gracious hand
    our humble prayers implore;
And Thou shalt be our chosen God,
    and portion evermore.

                              Michael Bruce

60   The Hour of my Departure's come

The hour of my departure's come;
I hear the voice that calls me home
At last, O Lord! let trouble cease,
And let thy servant die in peace.

The race appointed I have run;
The combat's o'er, the prize is won;
And now my witness is on high,
And now my record's in the sky.

GOD AND MAN   67

Not in mine innocence I trust;
I bow before thee in the dust;
And through my Saviour's blood alone
I look for mercy at thy throne.

I leave the world without a tear,
Save for the friends I held so dear;
To heal their sorrows, Lord, descend,
And to the friendless prove a friend.

I come, I come, at thy command,
I give my spirit to thy hand;
Stretch forth thine everlasting arms,
And shield me in the last alarms.

The hour of my departure's come;
I hear the voice that calls me home:
Now, O my God! let trouble cease;
Now let Thy servant die in peace.

Michael Bruce

61   A Prayer under the Pressure of violent Anguish

O Thou Great Being! what Thou art,
    Surpasses me to know:
Yet sure I am, that known to Thee
    Are all Thy works below.

Thy creature here before Thee stands,
    All wretched and distrest;
Yet sure those ills that wring my soul
    Obey Thy high behest.

Sure Thou, Almighty, canst not act
    From cruelty or wrath!
O, free my weary eyes from tears,
    Or close them fast in death!

GOD AND MAN

But if I must afflicted be,
    To suit some wise design,
Then man my soul with firm resolves
    To bear and not repine!

Robert Burns

62   Winter: a Dirge

The wintry West extends his blast,
    And hail and rain does blaw;
Or, the stormy North sends driving forth
    The blinding sleet and snaw:
While, tumbling brown, the Burn comes down,
    And roars frae bank to brae;
And bird and beast, in covert, rest,
    And pass the heartless day.

'The sweeping blast, the sky o'ercast,'
    The joyless winter day,
Let others fear, to me more dear
    Than all the pride of May:
The Tempest's howl, it soothes my soul,
    My griefs it seems to join;
The leafless trees my fancy please,
    Their fate resembles mine!

Thou Pow'r Supreme whose mighty scheme
    These woes of mine fulfil;
Here firm I rest, they *must* be best,
    Because they are *Thy* Will!
Then all I want (Oh do Thou grant
    This one request of mine!)
Since to *enjoy* Thou dost deny,
    Assist me to *resign!*

Robert Burns

'The sweeping blast' – a reference to Edward Young, 'Ocean: an Ode'.

O Thou unknown, Almighty Cause
   Of all my hope and fear!
In whose dread Presence, ere an hour,
   Perhaps I must appear!

If I have wander'd in those paths
   Of life I ought to shun;
As *Something,* loudly, in my breast,
   Remonstrates I have done;

Thou know'st that Thou hast formed me,
   With Passions wild and strong;
And list'ning to their witching voice
   Has often led me wrong.

Where human *weakness* has come short,
   Or *frailty* stept aside,
Do Thou, All-Good — for such Thou art —
   In shades of darkness hide.

Where with *intention* I have err'd,
   No other plea I have,
But, *Thou art good;* and Goodness still
   Delighteth to forgive.

Robert Burns

Part II — Love and Its Changes

64   Jocky fou, Jenny fain

Jocky fou, Jenny fain,
Jenny was nae ill to gain,
She was couthy, he was kind,
And thus the wooer tell'd his mind:

'Jenny, I'll nae mair be nice,
Gi'e me love at ony price;
I winna prig for red or whyt,
Love alane can gi'e delyt.

Others seek they kenna what,
In looks, in carriage, and a' that;
Gi'e me love, for her I court:
Love in love makes a' the sport.

Colours mingl'd unco fine,
Common motives lang sinsyne,
Never can engage my love,
Until my fancy first approve.

It is na meat but appetite
That makes our eating a delyt;
Beauty is at best deceit;
Fancy only kens nae cheat.'

fou – full; *fain* – eager; *couthy* – loving; *nice* – fastidious; *gi'e* – give; *ony* – any;
prig – haggle; *kenna* – don't know; *unco* – excessively; *sinsyne* – since then.

65   In yon Garden fine an' gay

In yon garden fine and gay,
Picking lilies a' the day,
Gathering flowers o' ilka hue,
I wistna then what love could do.

Where love is planted there it grows;
It buds and blows like any rose;

It has a sweet and pleasant smell;
No flower on earth can it excel.

I put my hand into the bush,
    And thought the sweetest rose to find;
But pricked my finger to the bone,
    And left the sweetest rose behind.

a' — all; *ilka* — every; *wistna* — knew not.

66   Mary Morison

O Mary, at thy window be,
    It is the wish'd, the trysted hour!
Those smiles and glances let me see,
    That make the miser's treasure poor:
How blythely wad I bide the stoure,
    A weary slave frae sun to sun;
Could I the rich reward secure,
    The lovely Mary Morison.

Yestreen when to the trembling string
    The dance gaed thro' the lighted ha',
To thee my fancy took its wing,
    I sat, but neither heard, nor saw:
Though this was fair, and that was braw,
    And yon the toast of a' the town,
I sigh'd, and said amang them a',
    'Ye are na Mary Morison.'

Oh, Mary, canst thou wreck his peace,
    Wha for thy sake wad gladly die!
Or canst thou break that heart of his,
    Whase only faute is loving thee!
If love for love thou wilt na gie,
    At least be pity to me shown;
A thought ungentle canna be
    The thought o' Mary Morison.

                                  Robert Burns

trysted hour — hour of rendezvous; *stoure* — struggle; *frae* — from; *yestreen* —
yesterday evening; *gaed* — went; *ha'* — hall; *braw* — finely dressed; *na* — not; *faute* —
fault; *gie* — give.

67   Dunt, dunt, pittie, pattie

On Whitsunday morning
  I went to the fair,
My yellow-hair'd laddie
  Was selling his ware;
He gied me sic a blyth blink
  With his bonny black eye,
And a dear blink, and a fair blink
  It was unto me.

I wist not what ail'd me
  When my laddie came in,
The little wee starnies
  Flew ay frae my een;
And the sweat it dropt down
  Frae my very eye-brie,
And my heart play'd ay
  Dunt, dunt, dunt, pittie, pattie.

I wist not what ail'd me,
  When I went to my bed,
I tossed and tumbled
  And sleep frae me fled.
Now its sleeping and waking
  He is ay in my eye;
And my heart play'd ay
  Dunt, dunt, dunt, pittie, pattie.

dunt – thump; *gied* – gave; *wist* – knew; *starnies* – stars; *ay* – continually; *frae* – from; *eye-brie* – eyebrow.

68   Wat and weary

O wat, wat – O wat and weary!
Sleep I can get nane

For thinking on my deary.
A' the night I wak,
A' the day I weary,
Sleep I can get nane
For thinking on my dearie.

wat — wet; *nane* — none; *a'* — all.

69   O my Love's bonny

O if my love was a pickle of wheat
And growing upon yon lilly-white lee,
And I myself a bonny sweet bird:
Away with that pickle I wad flie.
    O my love's bonny, bonny, bonny,
    My love's bonny and fair to see.

O if my love was a bonny red rose
And growing upon some barren wa',
And I myself a drap of dew:
Down in that red rose I would fa'.
    O my love's bonny, etc.

O if my love was a coffer of gold,
And I the keeper of the key:
Then I would open it when I lest,
And into that coffer I would be.
    O my love's bonny, etc.

pickle — grain; *lee* — meadow; *wa'* — wall; *drap* — drop; *lest* — pleased.

70   Slighted Nancy

'Tis I have seven braw new gowns,
    And ither seven better to mak;
And yet for a' my new gowns,
    My wooer has turn'd his back.

Besides, I have seven milk ky,
   And Sandy he has but three;
And yet for a' my good ky,
   The laddie winna ha'e me.

My dady's a delver of dikes,
   My mither can card and spin,
And I am a fine fodgel lass,
   And the siller comes linkin in:
The siller comes linkin in,
   And it is fou fair to see,
And fifty times wow! O wow!
   What ails the lads at me?

When ever our Baty does bark,
   Then fast to the door I rin,
To see gin ony young spark
   Will light and venture but in:
But never a ane will come in,
   Tho' mony a ane gaes by,
Syne far ben the house I rin;
   And a weary wight am I.

When I was at my first pray'rs,
   I pray'd but anes i' the year,
I wish'd for a handsome young lad,
   And a lad with muckle gear.
When I was at my neist pray'rs,
   I pray'd but now and than,
I fash'd na my head about gear,
   If I got a handsome young man.

Now when I'm at my last pray'rs,
   I pray on baith night and day,
And O! if a beggar wad come,
   With that same beggar I'd gae.
And O! and what'll come o' me?
   And O! and what'll I do?
That sic a braw lassie as I
   Shou'd die for a wooer I trow.

                        Allan Ramsay

71   Oh wert Thou in the cauld Blast

Oh wert thou in the cauld blast,
     On yonder lea, on yonder lea;
My plaidie to the angry airt,
     I'd shelter thee, I'd shelter thee:
Or did misfortune's bitter storms
     Around thee blaw, around thee blaw,
Thy bield should be my bosom,
     To share it a', to share it a'.

Or were I in the wildest waste,
     Sae black and bare, sae black and bare,
The desert were a Paradise,
     If thou wert there, if thou wert there.
Or were I monarch o' the globe,
     Wi' thee to reign, wi' thee to reign,
The brightest jewel in my crown,
     Wad be my queen, wad be my queen.

Robert Burns

cauld − cold; *lea* − meadow; *plaidie* − plaid; *airt* − direction (of wind); *blaw* − blow; *bield* − shelter; *wad* − would.

72   Some say that Kissing's a Sin

Some say that kissing's a sin,
    But I say that winna stand:
It is a most innocent thing,
    And allow'd by the laws of the land.

If it were a transgression,
    The ministers it would reprove;
But they, their elders and session,
    Can do it as weel as the lave.

Its lang since it came in fashion,
    I'm sure it will never be done,
As lang as there's in the nation
    A lad, lass, wife, or a lown.

What can I say more to commend it,
    Tho' I should speak all my life?
Yet this will I say in the end o't,
    Let ev'ry man kiss his ain wife.

Let him kiss her, clap her, and dawt her,
    And gie her benevolence due,
And that will a thrifty wife mak her,
    And sae I'll bid farewell to you.

winna – won't; *session* – meeting of parish elders; *weel* – well; *lave* – remainder; *lang* –
long; *lown* – fellow; *ain* – own; *clap* – embrace; *dawt* – caress; *gie* – give; *sae* – so.

73   Kissin is the Key o' Love

Kissin is the key o' love
    An' clappin' is the lock
An' makin o's the best thing
    That ere a young thing got.

Kissin is the Key – sung by Burns's mother; *makin o's* – heavy petting.

John, come kiss me now, now, now,
  O John come kiss me now;
John come kiss me by and by,
  And make nae mair ado.

Some will court and compliment,
  And make a great ado,
Some will make of their goodman,
  And sae will I of you.
John, come kiss, etc.

ado – fuss; *make of* – fondle; *goodman* – husband.

75   When I gaed to the Mill

When I gaed to the mill my lane,
  For to ground my malt,
The miller-laddie kist me,
  I thought it was nae fau't.
What tho' the laddie kist me,
  When I was at the mill?
A kiss is but a touch,
  And a touch can do nae ill!

O I lue the miller-laddie,
  And my laddie lues me,
He has sic a blyth look,
  And a bonie, blinking ee!
What tho' the laddie kist me,
  When I was at the mill?
A kiss is but a touch,
  And a touch can do nae ill.

my lane – by myself; *nae* – no; *fau't* – fault; *lue* – love; *sic* – such; *ee* – eye. (In the original, *laddie* is consistently spelt *ladie*, which presumably indicates a long vowel sound.)

76 Kiss ye, Jean

Kiss ye, Jean, kiss ye, Jean,
Never let an auld man kiss ye, Jean!
And auld man's nae man till a young quean:
Never let an auld man kiss ye, Jean!

auld – old; *nae* – no; *till* – to; *quean* – girl.

77 Kist the Streen

O as I was kist the streen!
O as I was kist the streen!
I'll never forget till the day that I die,
Sae mony braw kisses his Grace ga'e me.

My father was sleeping, my mither was out,
And I was my lane, and in came the duke,
I'll never forget till the day that I die,
Sae mony braw kisses his Grace ga'e me.

Kist the streen, kist the streen
Up the Gallowgate, down the green:
I'll never forget till the day that I die,
Sae mony braw kisses his Grace ga'e me.

Kist the Streen – said to have been written about John, Duke of Argyll; *the streen* –
yesterday evening; *mony* – many; *braw* – fine; *ga'e* – gave; *my lane* – alone; *up the
Gallowgate, down the green* – favourite walk of Glasgow lads and lasses, referring to
places within the city.

78 Bonie Peggy Alison

> *Chorus*
> *An I'll kiss thee yet, yet,*
>   *An I'll kiss thee o'er again;*
> *An I'll kiss thee yet, yet,*
>   *My bony Peggy Alison.*

THE KISS 81

Ilk Care and Fear, when thou art near,
   I evermair defy them, O!
Young kings upon their hansel throne
   Are no sae blest as I am, O!
     An I'll kiss thee etc.

When in my arms, wi' a' thy charms,
   I clasp my countless treasure, O!
I seek nae mair o' Heav'n to share,
   Than sic a moment's pleasure, O!
     An I'll kiss thee etc.

And by thy een sae bony blue,
   I swear I'm thine for ever, O!
And on thy lips I seal my vow,
   And break it shall I never, O!
     An I'll kiss thee etc.

                          Robert Burns

ilk – every; *hansel* – good-luck gift; *sic* – such; *een* – eyes.

THE KISS

79   Why Betty's Coy

My naked beauty thus display'd
    Unguarded from thy wanton hand,
May be sufficient to persuade
    I wish to be at thy command.

But, gentle Strephon, pray forbear
    To press the argument so strong,
And let me whisper in your ear
    Why I refuse the joy so long.

It is not to secure a fame
    (That empty purchase I give o'er);
For, happy to deserve the name,
    I grudge not to be call'd thy whore.

But rather, as most lovers are,
    After enjoyment you grow cold,
And we poor wretches still must fear
    To be abandon'd when we're old.

                    Alexander Robertson of Struan

Why Betty's Coy – the second part of a dialogue that begins with a conventional
request that she yield, beginning 'Betty, 'tis foolish to deny.'

80   John Anderson, my Jo

John Anderson, my jo, John,
    I wonder what ye mean,
To lie sae lang i' the mornin',
    And sit sae late at e'en?
Ye'll bleer a' your een, John,
    And why do ye so?
Come sooner to your bed at een,
    John Anderson, my jo.

John Anderson, my jo, John,
    When first that ye began,
Ye had as good a tail-tree,
    As ony ither man;
But now it's waxen wan, John,
    And wrinkles to and fro;
I've twa gae-ups for ae gae-down,
    John Anderson, my jo.

I'm backit like a salmon,
    I'm breastit like a swan;
My wame it is a down-cod,
    My middle ye may span:
Frae my tap-knot to my tae, John,
    I'm like the new-fa'n snow;
And it's a' for your convenience,
    John Anderson, my jo.

O it is a fine thing
    To keep out o'er the dyke;
But it's a meikle finer thing,
    To see your hurdies fyke;
To see your hurdies fyke, John,
    And hit the rising blow;
It's then I like your chanter-pipe,
    John Anderson, my jo.

When ye come on before, John,
    See that ye do your best;
When ye begin to haud me,
    See that ye grip me fast;
See that ye grip me fast, John,
    Until that I cry 'Oh!'
Your back shall crack or I do that,
    John Anderson, my jo.

John Anderson, my jo, John,
    Ye're welcome when ye please;
It's either in the warm bed
    Or else aboon the claes:

                                           SENSUAL LOVE

Or ye shall hae the horns, John,
    Upon your head to grow;
An' that's the cuckold's mallison,
    John Anderson, my jo.

jo – sweetheart; *e'en* – evening; *een* – eyes; *tail-tree* – penis; *gae* – go; *cod* – pillow;
tap-knot – bow of ribbon worn on top of head; *tae* – toe; *keep* – receive, hold in
possession; *out o'er* – quite over; *dyke* – ditch, wall (euphemism); *meikle* – much;
hurdies – buttocks; *fyke* – twitch; *chanter-pipe* – finger pipe of bagpipe (euphemism);
haud – hold; *or* – before; *mallison* – curse.

81   The Lass that made the Bed

When Januar wind was blawing cauld
    As to the north I took my way,
The mirksome night did me enfauld,
    I knew na whare to lodge till day.

By my gude luck a maid I met,
    Just in the middle o' my care;
And kindly she did me invite
    To walk into a chamber fair.

I bow'd fu' low unto this maid,
    And thank'd her for her courtesie;
I bow'd fu' low unto this maid,
    An' bade her make a bed for me.

She made the bed baith large and wide,
    Wi' twa white hands she spread it down;
She put the cup to her rosy lips
    And drank, 'Young man, now sleep ye sound.'

She snatch'd the candle in her hand,
    And frae my chamber went wi' speed;
But I call'd her quickly back again,
    To lay some mair below my head. –

A cod she laid below my head,
    And served me with due respect;
And, to salute her wi' a kiss,
    I put my arms about her neck.

SENSUAL LOVE   85

'Haud aff your hands, young man!' she says,
  'And dinna sae uncivil be:
Gif ye hae ony luve for me,
  O wrang na my virginitie!'

Her hair was like the links o' gowd,
  Her teeth were like the ivorie,
Her cheeks like lillies dipt in wine,
  The lass that made the bed to me.

Her bosom was the driven snaw,
  Twa drifted heaps sae fair to see;
Her limbs the polish'd marble stane,
  The lass that made the bed to me.

I kiss'd her o'er and o'er again,
  And aye she wist na what to say;
I laid her between me and the wa',
  The lassie thocht na lang till day.

Upon the morrow when we raise,
  I thank'd her for her courtesie:
But aye she blush'd, and aye she sigh'd,
  And said, 'Alas, ye've ruin'd me.'

I clasp'd her waist, and kiss'd her syne,
  While the tear stood twinklin in her e'e;
I said, 'My lassie, dinna cry,
  For ye aye shall make the bed to me.'

She took her mither's holland sheets
  And made them a' in sarks to me:
Blythe and merry may she be,
  The lass that made the bed to me.

Chorus
The bonie lass made the bed to me,
The braw lass made the bed to me;
I'll ne'er forget till the day that I die,
The lass that made the bed to me.

                              Robert Burns

mirksome – darksome *fu'* – full; *baith* – both; *twa* – two; *cod* – pillow; *haud* – hold;
dinna – don't; *sae* – so; *gif* – if; *gowd* – gold; *snaw* – snow; *wish* – knew; *na* – not; *syne*
– then; *holland* – linen cloth; *sarks* – shirts.

SENSUAL LOVE

82   O gin I had her

O gin I had her,
Ay gin I had her,
O gin I had her,
    Black altho' she be.
I wad lay her bale,
I'd gar her spew her kail;
She ne'er sould keep a mail
    Till she dandl'd it on her knee.

gin – if; *black* – i.e. dark-haired; *lay her bale* – put down her bundle; *gar* – make;
kail – colewort or cabbage soup; *keep a mail* – ? keep her food down/atone by paying
'buttock mail' or fee for fornication.

83   Lass, an I come near thee

Lass, an I come near thee
Lass, an I come near thee
I'll gar a' your ribbons reel,
Lass, an I come near thee.

an – if; *gar* – make.

84   Wha is that at my Bower Door

'Wha is that at my bower door?'
    'O wha is it but Findlay!'
'Then gae your gate, ye'se nae be here!'
    'Indeed maun I,' quo' Findlay.

'What mak ye, sae like a thief?'
    'O come and see,' quo' Findlay;
'Before the morn ye'll work mischief:'
    'Indeed will I,' quo' Findlay.

'Gif I rise and let you in' —
  'Let me in,' quo' Findlay;
'Ye'll keep me waukin wi' your din:'
  'Indeed will I,' quo' Findlay;

'In my bower if ye should stay' —
  'Let me stay,' quo' Findlay;
'I fear ye'll bide till break o' day:'
  'Indeed will I,' quo' Findlay.

'Here this night if ye remain' —
  'I'll remain,' quo' Findlay;
'I dread ye'll learn the gate again;'
  'Indeed will I,' quo' Findlay.

'What may pass within this bower' —
  'Let it pass,' quo' Findlay;
'Ye maun conceal till your last hour:'
  'Indeed will I,' quo' Findlay.

                                        Robert Burns

gae — go; *gate* — way; *ye'se nae* — you shall not; *maun* — must; *mak* — do; *sae* — so;
gif — if; *waukin* — awake.

85   Yestreen I had a Pint o' Wine

Yestreen I had a pint o' wine,
  A place where body saw na;
Yestreen lay on this breast o' mine
  The gowden locks of Anna.
The hungry Jew in wilderness,
  Rejoicing o'er his manna,
Was naething to my hinnie bliss
  Upon the lips of Anna.

Ye monarchs, take the East and West
  Frae Indus to Savannah!
Gie me, within my straining grasp,
  The melting form of Anna.

There I'll despise Imperial charms,
    An Empress or Sultana,
While dying raptures in her arms
    I give and take with Anna!

Awa, thou flaunting God of Day!
    Awa, thou pale Diana!
Ilk star, gae hide thy twinkling ray,
    When I'm to meet my Anna!
Come, in thy raven plumage, Night,
    Sun, Moon, and Stars, withdrawn a';
And bring an angel pen to write
    My transports wi' my Anna!

Postscript
The Kirk an' State may join, an' tell
    To do sic things I mauna:
The Kirk an' State may gae to hell,
    And I'll gae to my Anna.
She is the sunshine o' my e'e,
    To live but her I canna;
Had I on earth but wishes three,
    The first should be my Anna.

Robert Burns

Anna — traditionally Anne Park, niece of the hostess of the Globe Inn, Dumfries; *yestreen* — last night; *na* — not; *gowden* — golden; *frae* — from; *gie* — give; *ilk* — each; *gae* — go; *a'* — all; *sic* — such; *e'e* — eye. (The postscript, 'by another', is in the *Merry Muses of Caledonia.)*

86   Jenny Nettles

Saw ye Jenny Nettles,
    Jenny Nettles, Jenny Nettles,
Saw ye Jenny Nettles
    Coming frae the market?
Bag and baggage on her back,
    Her fee and bountith in her lap;
Bag and baggage on her back,
    And a babie in her oxter?

I met ayont the kairny,
    Jenny Nettles, Jenny Nettles,
Singing till her bairny,
    Robin Rattle's bastard;
To flee the dool upo' the stool,
    And ilka ane that mocks her,
She round about seeks Robin out,
    To stap it in his oxter.

Fy, fy! Robin Rattle,
    Robin Rattle, Robin Rattle;
Fy, fy! Robin Rattle,
    Use Jenny Nettles kindly:
Score out the blame, and shun the shame,
    And without mair debate o't,
Tak hame your wean, make Jenny fain
    The leel and leesome gate o't.

                                    Allan Ramsay

frae – from; *fee and bountith* – wages and gratuity; *oxter* – crook of arm; *kairny* –
heap of stones; *till* – to; *dool* – misery; *stool* – i.e. of repentance; *ilka ane* –
everyone; *stap* – stuff; *mair* – more; *wean* – child; *fain* – glad; *leel* – true; *leesome*
– compassionate; *gate* – way.

O wha my babie-clouts will buy?
O wha will tent me when I cry?
Wha will kiss me where I lie?
  The rantin dog the daddie o't.

O wha will own he did the faut?
O wha will buy the groanin maut?
O wha will tell me how to ca't?
  The rantin dog the daddie o't.

When I mount the creepie-chair,
Wha will sit beside me there?
Gie me Rob, I'll seek nae mair,
  The rantin dog the daddie o't.

Wha will crack to me my lane?
Wha will mak me fidgin fain?
Wha will kiss me o'er again?
  The rantin dog the daddie o't.

                                        Robert Burns

-clouts – clothes; *tent* – take care of; *faut* – fault; *groanin maut* – ale for the midwife and her friends; *ca't* – name it; *creepie-chair* – stool of repentance in parish church on which fornicators had to sit; *crack* – chat; *my lane* – alone; *fidgin fain* – tingling with delight.

THE CONSEQUENCES

88   An Ode inscribed to King William

To hide their pastime from the sun,
    Stretch'd in a gloomy grove,
Alexis lay with Corydon
    Like Ganymede with Jove.

The amorous swain relates with grief
    Love's lamentable story,
And little Alexis gave belief
    To all was told by Cory.

Sighing, said he, 'Alone 'tis you
    Can bless my inclination;'
But what the shepherd meant to do
    Is needless here to mention.

Yet in the sequel, we may find
    The younker was not cruel,
And that a swain so very kind
    Fed not water-gruel.

Fair Amaryllis, passing by,
    A nose had like a terrier;
Soon smelt them out, and saw them lie
    Like Venus with the warrior.

Just as the swain had tun'd his pipe,
    And all his courting ended,
When the love-plot was fully ripe,
    She spoil'd what they intended.

Dire jealousy her rage provok'd
    To most unchristian wishes;
She could have seen Alexis chok'd,
    And Cory torn to pieces!

'Tell me,' quoth she, 'what do you see
    In him the De'il has sent ye,

But what you know possess'd by me,
    And that in greater plenty.

My Buttocks often to your cost,'
    And then she clapt her thigh, Sir,
'And sure your pathick cannot boast
    An arse so fair as I, Sir.

But since 'tis vain for me to rail,
    To make you change your fancy,
I'll in my turn go wag my tail,
    With Chloe's little Nancy.

Think not but we have active maids,
    As you have passive boys, Sir,
To ease us with less dangerous aids,
    And give more lasting joys, Sir.'

'Agreed,' quoth Cory, 'let's embrace;
    Henceforth let nothing vex us,
Go you, take Nancy in my place,
    I'll take in your's Alexis.'

Thus parted Corydon with her,
    To whom he once was cully;
And to old Jamie's does prefer
    A mode brought in by Willy.

                  Alexander Robertson of Struan

King William — William III (of Orange), reputed to be a homosexual; *De'il* — devil;
pathick — pervert; *cully* — man-friend; *Jamie* — James VII and II, unambiguously
heterosexual. (The first two lines of st. 9 seem textually corrupt.)

89   Rare Willy drown'd in Yarrow

Willy's rare, and Willy's fair,
    And Willy's wondrous bony,
And Willy hecht to marry me,
    Gin e'er he married ony.

Yestreen I made my bed fu' braid,
    This night I'll make it narrow;
For a' the live-lang winter night
    I'll lie twin'd of my marrow.

O came you by yon water side?
    Pou'd you the rose or lilly?
Or came you by yon meadow green?
    Or saw ye my sweet Willy?

She sought him east, she sought him west,
    She sought him braid and narrow;
Syne in the cleaving of a craig,
    She found him drown'd in Yarrow.

hecht – promised; *yestreen* – yesterday evening; *fu'* – full; *braid* – broad; *twin'd of* –
separated from; *syne* – then; *craig* – rock.

90   It's open the Door, some Pity to show

'It's open the door, some pity to show,
It's open the door to me, oh!
Though you have been false, I'll always prove true,
So open the door to me, oh!

Cold is the blast upon my pale cheek,
But colder your love unto me, oh!
Though you have been false, I'll always prove true,
So open the door to me, oh!'

She's open'd the door, she's open'd it wide,
She sees his pale corps on the ground, oh!
Though you have been false, I'll always prove true,
So open the door to me, oh!

'My true love!' she cry'd, then fell down by his side,
Never, never to rise again, oh!
Though you have been false, I'll always prove true,
So open the door to me, oh!

91   Oh, on o chri o

O was not I a weary wight!
   Oh on o chri oh!
Maid, wife and widow in ane night.
   Oh on o chri oh!

When in my soft and yielding arms,
   Oh on o chri oh!
When most I thought him free from harms,
   Oh on o chri oh!

Even at the dead time of the night,
   Oh on o chri oh!
They broke my bower and slew my knight,
   Oh on o chri oh!

With ae lock of his jet black hair,
   Oh on o chri oh!
I'll tie my heart for ever mair.
   Oh on o chri oh!

Nae sly-tongu'd youth or flattering swain
   Oh on o chri oh!
Shall e'er untie this knot again.
   Oh on o chri oh!

Thine still, dear youth, that heart shall be,
   Oh on o chri oh!
Nor pant for aught save heaven and thee.
   On on o chri o!

ae – one.

THE PLAINTIVE STRAIN   95

Chorus

Canst thou leave me thus, my Katy?
Canst thou leave me thus, my Katy?
Well thou know'st my aching heart,
And canst thou leave me thus for pity?

Is this thy plighted, fond regard,
　　Thus cruelly to part, my Katy?
Is this thy faithful swain's reward —
　　An aching, broken heart, my Katy!
　　　　Canst thou etc.

Farewell! and ne'er such sorrows tear
　　That fickle heart of thine, my Katy!
Thou mayest find those will love thee dear —
　　But not a love like mine, my Katy!
　　　　Canst thou etc.

Robert Burns

93　　　　　Thou hast left me ever, Jamie

Thou hast left me ever, Jamie,
　　Thou hast left me. ever.
Thou hast left me ever, Jamie,
　　Thou hast left me ever.
Aften hast thou vow'd that Death,
　　Only should us sever:
Now thou's left thy lass for ay —
　　I maun see thee never, Jamie,
　　I'll see thee never.

Thou hast me forsaken, Jamie,
　　Thou hast me forsaken:
Thou hast me forsaken, Jamie,
　　Thou hast me forsaken.

Thou canst love anither jo,
   While my heart is breaking:
Soon my weary een I'll close —
   Never mair to waken, Jamie,
   Ne'er mair to waken!

Robert Burns

aye — ever; *maun* — must; *jo* — sweetheart; *een* — eyes.

94   Mary Scott

Happy's the love which meets return,
When in soft flames souls equal burn;
But words are wanting to discover
The torments of a hopeless lover.
Ye registers of heav'n, relate,
If looking o'er the rolls of fate,
Did you there see me mark'd to marrow
Mary Scott the flow'r of Yarrow?

Ah no! her form's too heav'nly fair,
Her love the gods above must share;
While mortals with despair explore her,
And at distance due adore her.
O lovely maid! my doubts beguile,
Revive and bless me with a smile:
Alas! if not, you'll soon debar a
Sighing swain the banks of Yarrow.

Be hush, ye fears, I'll not despair,
My Mary's tender as she's fair;
Then I'll go tell her all mine anguish,
She is too good to let me languish:
With success crown'd, I'll not envy
The folks who dwell above the sky;
When Mary Scott's become my marrow,
We'll make a paradise in Yarrow.

                                        Allan Ramsay

marrow – (vb.) marry, (n.) mate.

95   Tell me, Hamilla

Tell me, Hamilla, tell me why
    Thou dost from him that loves thee run?
Why from his soft embraces fly,
    And all his kind endearments shun?

So flies the fawn, with fear oppress'd,
    Seeking its mother ev'ry where,
It starts at ev'ry empty blast,
    And trembles when no danger's near.

And yet I keep thee but in view,
    To gaze the glories of thy face,
Not with a hateful step pursue,
    As age to rifle every grace.

Cease, then, dear wildness, cease to toy,
    But haste all rivals to outshine,
And grown mature, and ripe for joy,
    Leave mamma's arms, and come to mine.

William Hamilton of Bangour

Tell me, Hamilla – an imitation of Horace, *Odes* I, xxiii.

96   I'll never leave thee

One day I heard Mary say,
    How shall I leave thee?
Stay, dearest Adonis, stay,
    Why wilt thou grieve me?
Alas! my fond heart will break,
    If thou should leave me.
I'll live and die for thy sake:
    Yet never leave thee.

Say, lovely Adonis, say,
    Has Mary deceiv'd thee?
Did e'er her young heart betray
    New love, that has griev'd thee?
My constant mind ne'er shall stray,
    Thou may believe me.
I'll love thee, lad, night and day,
    And never leave thee.

Adonis, my charming youth,
    What can relieve thee?
Can Mary thy anguish sooth!
    This breast shall receive thee.
My passion can ne'er decay,
    Never deceive thee:
Delight shall drive pain away,
    Pleasure revive thee.

But leave thee, leave thee, lad,
    How shall I leave thee?
O! that thought makes me sad,
    I'll never leave thee.
Where would my Adonis fly?
    Why does he grieve me?
Alas! my poor heart will die,
    If I should leave thee.

                              Robert Crawford

97   Where are the Joys?

Where are the joys I have met in the morning,
    That danc'd to the lark's early song?
Where is the peace that awaited my wand'ring,
    At evening the wild-woods among?

No more a winding the course of yon river,
    And marking sweet flowerets so fair,
No more I trace the light footsteps of Pleasure,
    But Sorrow and sad-sighing Care.

Is it that Summer's forsaken our valleys,
    And grim, surly Winter is near?
No, no! the bees humming round the gay roses
    Proclaim it the pride of the year.

Fain would I hide, what I fear to discover,
    Yet long, long, too well have I known:
All that has caused this wreck in my bosom,
    Is Jenny, fair Jenny alone.

THE CULT OF SENTIMENT

Time cannot aid me, and griefs are immortal,
  Nor Hope dare a comfort bestow:
Come then, enamour'd and fond of my anguish,
  Enjoyment I'll seek in my woe.

Robert Burns

98   Throw the Wood, Laddie

O Sandy, why leaves thou thy Nelly to mourn?
  Thy presence could ease me,
  When naething can please me;
Now dowie I sigh on the bank of the burn,
Or throw the wood, laddie, until thou return.

Tho' woods now are bonny, and mornings are clear,
  While lav'rocks are singing,
  And primroses springing;
Yet nane of them pleases my eye or my ear,
When throw the wood, laddie, ye dinna appear.

That I am forsaken, some spare not to tell:
  I'm fash'd wi' their scorning,
  Baith ev'ning and morning;
Their jeering gaes aft to my heart wi' a knell,
When throw the wood, laddie, I wander mysell.

Then stay, my dear Sandy, nae langer away
  But quick as an arrow,
  Haste here to thy marrow,
Wha's living in languor till that happy day,
When throw the wood, laddie, we'll dance, sing and play.

                                        Allan Ramsay

dowie – doleful; burn – stream; lav'rocks – larks; dinna – don't; fash'd – vexed; baith
– both; aft – often; mysell – myself; marrow – mate.

99   I'll chear up my Heart

  As I was a walking ae May-morning,
The fidlers and youngsters were making their game,
And there I saw my faithless lover,
And a' my sorrows returned again.

Well, since he is gane, joy gang wi' him;
It's never be he shall gar me complain:
I'll chear up my heart, and I will get another,
I'll never lay a' my love upon ane.

I could na get sleeping yestreen for weeping,
The tears ran down like showers o' rain;
An' had na I got greiting my heart wad a broken;
And O! but love's a tormenting pain.

But since he is gane, may joy gae wi' him,
It's never be he that shall gar me complain,
I'll chear up my heart, and I will get another;
I'll never lay a' my love upon ane.

When I gade into my mither's new house,
I took my wheel and sate down to spin;
'Twas there I first began my thrift;
And a' the wooers came linking in.

It was gear he was seeking, but gear he'll na get;
And its never be he, that shall gar me complain,
For I'll chear up my heart, and I'll soon get another;
I'll never lay a' my love upon ane.

ae — one; *a'* — all; *gang* — go; *it's* — it shall; *gar* — make; *yestreen* — yesterday evening; *na* — not; *greiting* — weeping; *wad* — would; *gae* — go; *gade* — went; *linking* — tripping.

100   Joy gae down the Loaning wi' her

Joy gae down the Loaning wi' her
An joy gae down the Loaning wi' her;
She wadna hae me but she's taen anither,
An a man's joy but mine gae with her.

gae — go; *Loaning* — strip of grass running through arable field, serving as driving road; *hae* — have; *taen* — taken; *a man's* — all men's.

PARTING AND JILTING   103

Ae fond kiss, and then we sever;
Ae fareweel, and then for ever!
Deep in heart-wrung tears I'll pledge thee,
Warring sighs and groans I'll wage thee.

Who shall say that Fortune grieves him,
While the star of hope she leaves him?
Me, nae cheerful twinkle lights me;
Dark despair around benights me.

I'll ne'er blame my partial fancy,
Naething could resist my Nancy:
But to see her was to love her;
Love but her, and love for ever.

Had we never lov'd sae kindly,
Had we never lov'd sae blindly!
Never met — or never parted,
We had ne'er been broken-hearted.

Fare-thee-weel, thou first and fairest!
Fare-thee-weel, thou best and dearest!
Thine be ilka joy and treasure,
Peace, Enjoyment, Love and Pleasure!

Ae fond kiss, and then we sever!
Ae fareweel, Alas, for ever!
Deep in heart-wrung tears I'll pledge thee,
Warring sighs and groans I'll wage thee.

Robert Burns

ae — one; *ilka* — every.

102   Fee him, father, fee him

O saw ye Johny cumin, quo' she,
    Saw ye Johny cumin;
O saw ye Johny cumin, quo' she,
    Saw ye Johny cumin;
O saw ye Johny cumin, quo' she,
    Saw ye Johny cumin;
Wi' his blew bonnet on his head,
    And his dogie rinnin, quo' she,
    And his dogie rinnin?

O fee him, father, fee him, quo' she,
    Fee him, father, fee him;
O fee him, father, fee him, quo' she,
    Fee him, father, fee him;
For he is a gallant lad, and a weel-doin, quo' she,
    And a' the wark about the town
Gaes wi' me when I see him, quo' she,
Gaes wi' me when I see him.

O what will I do wi' him, quo' he,
    What will I do wi' him?
He has ne'er a coat upon his back,
    And I hae nane to gi'e him.
I hae twa coats into my kist,
    And ane of them I'll gi'e him;
And for a merk of mair fee
    Dinna stand wi' him, quo' she,
    Dinna stand wi' him.

For weel do I loe him, quo' she, weel do I loe him;
For weel do I loe him, quo' she, weel do I loe him.
O fee him, father, fee him, quo' she,
    Fee him, father, fee him;
He'll ha'd the pleugh, thrash in the barn,
    And crack wi' me at e'en, quo' she
    And crack wi' me at e'en.

fee – hire; *weel-doin* – well-conducted; *wark* – work; *gaes* – goes; *ha'e* – have; *nane* – none; *gi'e* – give; *kist* – chest; *mair* – more; *stand wi'* – take a firm stand against; *loe* – love; *ha'd* – hold; *pleugh* – plough; *crack* – chat; *e'en* – evening.

103   I gotten the Laddie that I liked sair

I gotten the Laddie that I liked sair,
I gotten the Laddie that I liked sair,
I gotten the Laddie that I liked sair
And I'll never lie wi' my auld minny nae mair.

The Har'est it is shorn the rigs they are bare,
The Har'est it is shorn the rigs they are bare,
The Har'est it is shorn the rigs they are bare,
And I'll never lie wi' my auld minny nae mair.

sair – passionately; *auld* – old; *minny* – mother; *nae mair* – no more; *rigs* – ridges.

104   I'll ha'e a Fiddler

I'll ha'e a fiddler to my goodman
I'll ha'e a fiddler to my goodman
If I dinnae get meat eneugh I'll get play,
And I'll get skeeg about a' the lang day.

ha'e – have; *goodman* – husband; *dinnae* – don't; *eneugh* – enough; *skeeg about* – rhythmic strokes.

105   There's a Lad i' the Town

There's a Lad i' the town has a fancy for me,
There's a Lad i' the town has a fancy for me,
But they're nearer my heart that's farer frae me,
An he's blacker that I lo'e better than he.

There's better an better providing for me,
There's better an better providing for me,
There's better an better providing for me,
There's a coach an six horses a riding for me.

farer – farther; *blacker* – darker (of hair); *lo'e* – love.

O Logie o' Buchan, O Logie the laird,
They ha'e ta'en awa' Jamie, that delved in the yard,
Wha play'd on the pipe, and the viol sae sma';
They ha'e ta'en awa' Jamie, the flower o' them a'.
   He said, Think na lang lassie, tho' I gang awa',
   He said, Think na lang lassie, tho' I gang awa';
   The simmer is come, and the winter's awa',
   And I'll come and see thee in spite o' them a'.

Tho' Sandy has owsen, and siller, and kye;
A house and a hadden, and a' things forbye:
Yet I'd tak' mine ain lad, wi' his staff in his hand,
Before I'd ha'e him, wi' the houses and land.
   He said, Think na lang, etc.

My daddie looks sulky, my minnie looks sour,
They frown upon Jamie because he is poor;
But daddie and minnie altho' that they be,
There's nane o' them a' like my Jamie to me.
   He said, Think na lang, etc.

I sit on my creepie, I spin at my wheel,
And think on my Jamie that lo'es me sae weel;
He had but ae saxpence, he brak it in twa,
And gi'ed me the hauf o't when he gade awa'.
   Then haste ye back, Jamie, and bide na awa',
   Then haste ye back, Jamie, and bide na awa';
   The simmer is come, and the winter's awa',
   And ye'll come and see me in spite o' them a'.

attrib. G. Halket

Logie — estate in Crimond Parish, Aberdeenshire; *laird* — landlord; *ta'en awa'* — taken
away (? to military service); *Jamie* — said to have been James Robertson, gardener on
the estate; *think na lang* — don't brood; *gang* — go; *owsen* — oxen; *siller* — money; *kye* —
cattle; *hadden* — holding; *forbye* — in addition; *ain* — own; *ha'e* — have; *minnie* —
mother; *nane* — none; *creepie* — low stool; *lo'es* — loves; *ae* — one; *gi'ed* — gave; *gade* —
went; *bide* — stay.

My daddy is a canker'd carle
  He'll nae twin wi' his gear;
My minny she's a scalding wife,
  Hads a' the house asteer;
    But let them say, or let them do,
     It's a' ane to me,
    For he's low down, he's in the broom,
     That's waiting on me:
    Waiting on me, my love,
     He's waiting on me;
    For he's low down, he's in the broom,
     That's waiting on me.

My aunty Kate sits at her wheel,
  And sair she lightlies me;
But weel ken I it's a' envy,
  For ne'er a jo has she;
    But let them say, etc.

My cousin Kate was sair beguil'd
  Wi' Johnny in the Glen;
And ay since syne she cries, Beware
  Of false deluding men;
    But let them say, etc.

Glee'd Sandy, he came west ae night,
  And speer'd when I saw Pate;
And aye since syne the neighbours round
  They jeer me air and late;
    But let them say, or let them do,
     It's a' ane to me,
    For he's low down, he's in the broom,
     That's waiting on me:
    Waiting on me, my love,
     He's waiting on me;
    For he's low down, he's in the broom,
     That's waiting on me.

canker'd carle — bad-tempered man; *twin* — part; *minny* — mother; *asteer* — in confusion; *a' ane* — all one; *sair* — vehemently; *lightlies* — disparages; *jo* — sweetheart; *aye since syne* — ever since then; *glee'd* — squint-eyed; *Sandy* — Alexander; *speer'd* — asked; *Pate* — Pete; *air* — early.

Chorus

O whistle, and I'll come to ye, my lad,
O whistle, and I'll come to ye, my lad,
Tho' father, and mother, and a' should gae mad,
Thy Jeanie will venture wi' ye, my lad.

But warily tent, when ye come to court me,
And come nae unless the back-yett be a-jee;
Syne up the back-style and let naebody see,
    And come as ye were na comin to me —
    And come as ye were na comin to me.
        O whistle etc.

At kirk, or at market whene'er ye meet me,
Gang by me as tho' that ye car'd nae a flie;
But steal me a blink o' your bonie black e'e,
    Yet look as ye were na lookin at me —
    Yet look as ye were na lookin at me.
        O whistle etc.

Ay vow and protest that ye care na for me,
And whyles ye may lightly my beauty a wee;
But court nae anither, tho' jokin ye be,
    For fear that she wyle your fancy frae me,
    For fear that she wyle your fancy frae me.
        O whistle etc.

                                    Robert Burns

a' – all; *gae* – go; *tent* – take heed; *nae* – not; *-yett* – gate; *a-jee* – ajar; *syne* – then;
gang – go; *flie* – fly; *blink* – glance; *e'e* – eye; *aye* – always; *whyles* – sometimes;
lightly – disparage; *wee* – little; *wyle* – entice.

109   Tam Glen

My heart is a-breaking, dear tittie,
    Some counsel unto me come len';
To anger them a' is a pity,
    But what will I do wi' Tam Glen?

I'm thinking, wi' sic a braw fellow,
　　In poortith I might mak a fen':
What care I in riches to wallow,
　　If I maunna marry Tam Glen?

There's Lowrie the Laird o' Dumeller,
　　'Gude day to you brute!' he comes ben:
He brags and he blaws o' his siller,
　　But when will he dance like Tam Glen!

My Minnie does constantly deave me,
　　And bids me beware o' young men;
They flatter, she says, to deceive me,
　　But wha can think sae o' Tam Glen?

My Daddie says, gin I'll forsake him,
　　He'd gie me gude hunder marks ten:
But, if it's ordain'd I maun take him,
　　O wha will I get but Tam Glen?

Yestreen at the Valentines' dealing,
　　My heart to my mou' gied a sten;
For thrice I drew ane without failing,
　　And thrice it was written , Tam Glen.

The last Halloween I was waukin
　　My droukit sark-sleeve, as ye ken;
His likeness cam up the house staukin,
　　And the very grey breeks o' Tam Glen!

Come counsel, dear tittie, don't tarry;
　　I'll gie you my bonie black hen,
Gif ye will advise me to marry
　　The lad I lo'e dearly, Tam Glen.

Robert Burns

tittie — sister; a' — all; sic — such; braw — fine; poortith — poverty; fen' — shift;
maunna — must not; ben — in; blaws — brags; siller — money; Minnie — mother;
deave — deafen; gin — if; yestreen — last night; mou' — mouth; gied — gave; sten —
spring; ane — one; waukin . . . droukit sark-sleeve — watching the sleeve of my wetted
shift in front of the fire, until the apparition of the man I am to marry comes and
turns the sleeve, as if to dry it; staukin — stalking; breeks —. breeches; gif — if; lo'e —
love.

　　　　　　　　　　　　　　　YOUNG GIRLS SINGING

110   The Mill, Mill – O

Beneath a green shade I fand a fair maid,
    Was sleeping sound and still – O;
A' lowan wi' love, my fancy did rove
    Around her with good will – O:
Her bosom I press'd; but sunk in her rest,
    She stir'd na my joy to spill – O:
While kindly she slept, close to her I crept,
    And kiss'd, and kiss'd her my fill – O.

Oblig'd by command in Flanders to land,
    T' employ my courage and skill – O,
Frae her quietly I staw, hoist sails and awa',
    For the wind blew fair on the bill – O.
Twa years brought me hame, where loud fraising fame
    Tald me with a voice right shrill – O,
My lass, like a fool, had mounted the stool,
    Nor kent wha had done her the ill – O.

Mair fond of her charms, with my son in her arms,
    I ferlying speer'd how she fell – O.
Wi' the tear in her eye, quoth she, 'Let me die,
    Sweet Sir, gin I can tell – O.'
Love gave the command, I took her by the hand,
    And bade her a' fears expel – O,
And nae mair look wan, for I was the man
    Wha had done her the deed mysell – O.

My bonny sweet lass, on the gowany grass,
    Beneath the Shilling-hill – O,
If I did offence, I'se make ye amends
    Before I leave Peggy's mill – O.
O the mill, mill – O, and the kill, kill – O,
    And the coggin of the wheel – O:
The sack and the sieve, a' that ye maun leave,
    And round with a sodger reel – O.

                                   Allan Ramsay

fand – found; *lowan* – glowing; *na* – not; *spill* – destroy; *staw* – stole; *awa'* – away; *bill* – narrow promontory; *twa* – two; *fraising* – strident; *stool* – i.e. of repentance, in the parish church, because she had had an illegitimate child; *kent* – known; *mair* – more; *ferlying* – wandering; *speer'd* – asked; *gin* – if; *a'* – all; *mysell* – myself; *gowany* – covered with daisies; *Shilling-hill* – where the chaff is winnowed from the corn; *I'se* – I shall; *kill* – kiln (for drying grain); *coggin* – furnishing with cogs; *maun* – must; *sodger* – soldier; *reel* – travel.

111   Love is the Cause of my Mourning

Beneath a green willow's sad ominous shade
A simple sweet youth extended was laid,
They asked what ail'd him, when sighing he said:
'O love is the cause of my mourning!

Long lov'd I a lady, fair, gentle and gay,
And thought myself loved for many a day,
But now she is married, is married away:
And love is the cause of my mourning!

And when deck'd as a bride to the kirk she did go,
With bride-men and maidens, with pomp and with show,
She smil'd in appearance – she smil'd, but was woe:
O love is the cause of my mourning!

And when I had seen my love taken to bed,
And when they all kiss'd the bridegroom and bride,
Heavens! thought I, and must he then lie by her side?
O love is the cause of my mourning!

Now dig me, companions, a grave dark and deep,
Lay a stone at my head and a turf at my feet,
And O, I'll lie down, and I'll take a long sleep,
Nor waken for ever and ever!'

Love is the Cause – this song is a Scottish variant of an English broadside of the late seventeenth century.

I had a horse, and I had nae mair,
    I gat him frae my daddy;
My purse was light, and my heart was sair,
    But my wit it was fu' ready.
And sae I thought upon a wile,
    Outwittens of my daddy,
To fee mysell to a lowland laird,
    Who had a bonny lady.

I wrote a letter, and thus began,
    'Madam, be not offended,
I'm o'er the lugs in love wi' you,
    And care not tho' ye kend it.
For I get little frae the laird,
    And far less frae my daddy,
And I would blythly be the man
    Would strive to please my lady.'

She read my letter, and she leuch,
    'Ye needna been sae blate, man;
You might hae come to me yoursell,
    And tald me o'your state man:
Ye might hae come to me yoursell,
    Outwittens of your daddy,
And made John Gouckston of the laird,
    And kiss'd his bonny lady.'

Then she pat siller in my purse,
    We drank wine in a cogie;
She fee'd a man to rub my horse,
    And wow but I was vogie:
But I gat ne'er sae sair a fleg
    Since I came frae my daddy,
The laird came rap rap to the yate,
    Whan I was wi' his lady.

Then she pat me below a chair,
    And hap'd me wi' a plaidie;
But I was like to swarf with fear,
    And wish'd me wi' my daddy.

TALES

The laird went out, he saw na me,
    I went whan I was ready:
I promis'd, but I ne'er gade back
    To see his bonny lady.

nae mair — no more; *frae* — from; *sair* — sore; *fu'* — full; *sae* — so; *outwittens of* — without the knowledge of; *fee* — hire; *laird* — landlord; *lugs* — ears; *kend* — knew; *leuch* — laughed; *needna* — need not [have]; *blate* — bashful; *John Gouckston of* — i.e., a fool of; *siller* — money; *cogie* — wooden drinking vessel; *vogie* — vain; *fleg* — fright; *yate* — gate; *pat* — put; *hap'd* — wrapped; *swarf* — swoon; *gade* — went.

113   My Lord a-hunting

My Lord a-hunting he is gane,
But hounds or hawks wi' him are nane;
By Colin's cottage lies his game,
If Colin's Jenny be at hame.

> *Chorus*
> *My Lady's gown, there's gairs upon't,*
> *And gowden flowers sae rare upon't;*
> *But Jenny's jimps and jirkenet,*
> *My lord thinks meikle mair upon't.*

My Lady's white, my Lady's red,
And kith and kin o' Cassillis' blude;
But her ten-pund lands o' tocher gude
Were a' the charms his Lordship lo'ed.
    My Lady's gown, etc.

Out o'er yon muir, out o'er yon moss,
Whare gor-cocks thro' the heather pass,
There wons auld Colin's bonie lass,
A lily in a wilderness.
    My Lady's gown, etc.

Sae sweetly move her genty limbs,
Like music-notes o' lovers' hymns;
The diamond-dew in her een sae blue,
Where laughing love sae wanton swims.
    My Lady's gown, etc.

My Lady's dink, my Lady's drest,
The flower and fancy o' the west;
But the Lassie that a man lo'es best,
O that's the lass to mak him blest.
  My Lady's gown, etc.

Robert Burns

gane — gone; *nane* — none; *gairs* — gussets; *gowden* — golden; *jimps* — skirts; *jirkenet* —
substitute for stays, without whalebone; *meikle* — much; *mair* — more; *Cassillis* —
aristocratic family in Ayrshire; *tocher gude* — dowry; *lo'ed* — loved; *gor-cocks* — red
grouse; *wons* — dwells; *sae* — so; *genty* — slender; *dink* — trim.

114   Go to the Kye wi' me, Johnny

'Go to the Kye wi me, Johnny,
Go to the Kye wi me,
Go to the Kye wi me, Johnny –
I'll go to the Kirk wi thee.

I kiss'd ye Johnny,
An I settin ye free;
I kiss'd ye, Johnny,
An winnae ye marry me.'

'Ye hae kiss'd me, Jenny,
An ye settin me free;
But had ye a thousand merk mair,
Ye s'oud never be married for me.

I ha'e a house a bigging
Anither like to fa;
And I ha'e a lass wi' Bairn
Which grieves maist of a.'

kye – cattle; *settin free* – i.e. from engagement; *an winnae* – if you won't; *merk* –
old silver coin worth thirteen and one-third pence sterling; *mair* – more; *s'oud* –
should; *bigging* – building; *fa* – fall; *Bairn* – child; *maist of a* – most of all.

115   Jocky said to Jeany

Jocky said to Jeany, 'Jeany, wilt thou do't?'
'Ne'er a fit,' quo' Jeany, 'for my tocher-good,
For my tocher-good, I winna marry thee.'
'E'ens ye like,' quo' Jocky, 'ye may let it be.

I hae gowd and gear, I hae land enough,
I hae seven good owsen ganging in a pleugh,
Ganging in a pleugh, and linking o'er the lee,
And gin ye winna tak me, I can let ye be.

I hae a good ha' house, a barn and a byre,
A stack afore the door, I'll make a rantin fire,
I'll make a rantin fire, and merry shall we be:
And gin ye winna tak me, I can let ye be.'

Jeany said to Jocky, 'Gin ye winna tell,
Ye shall be the lad, I'll be the lass mysell.
Ye're a bonny lad, and I'm a lassie free,
Ye're welcomer to tak me than to let me be.'

fit − foot; *for my tocher-good* − because of my dowry; *winna* − won't; *e'ens* − even as; *gowd* − gold; *owsen* − oxen; *ganging in a pleugh* − ploughing; *linking* − skipping; *lee* − meadow; *gin* − if; *ha' house* − substantial farmhouse; *afore* − before; *rantin* − jolly.

116   The linkin' Laddie

'Waes me that e'er I made your bed!
    Waes me that e'er I saw ye!
For now I've lost my maidenhead,
    An' I ken na how they ca' ye.'

'My name's weel kend in my ain countrie,
    They ca' me the linkin' laddie;
An' ye had na been as willing as I,
    Shame fa' them wad e'er hae bade ye.'

waes − woe is; *ken na* − don't know; *ca'* − name; *countrie* − region; *linkin'* − brisk; *an'* − if; *fa'* − befall; *hae bade* − have asked.

117   Supper is na ready

Roseberry to his lady says,
    'My hinnie and my succour,
'O shall we do the thing you ken,
    Or shall we take our supper?'
    Fal, lal, etc.

Wi' modest face, sae fu' o' grace,
    Replied the bonny lady;
'My noble lord do as you please,
    But supper is na ready.'
    Fal, lal, etc.

Roseberry — i.e. Lord Roseberry; *hinnie* — honey; *ken* — know.

118   O fair Maid, whase aught that bonny Bairn?

'O fair maid, whase aught that bonny bairn,
O fair maid, whase aught that bonny bairn?' —
'It is a sodger's son,' she said,
'That's lately gone to Spain.'
    Te dilly dan, te dilly dan, te dilly dilly dan.

'O fair maid, what was that sodger's name
O fair maid, what was that sodger's name?' —
'In troth I't will I never spear,
The mair I was to blame.'
Te dilly etc.

'O fair maid, what had that sodger on,
O fair maid, what had that sodger on?' —
'A scarlet coat laid o'er wi' gold,
A waistcoat o' the same.'
Te dilly etc.

'O fair maid, what if he should be slain,
O fair maid, what if he should be slain?' —
'The King would lose a brave sodger
And I a pretty man.'
Te dilly etc.

'O fair maid, what if he should come hame,
O fair maid, what if he should come hame?' —
'The parish priest should marry us,
The clerk should say amen.'
Te dilly etc.

'O fair maid, would ye that sodger ken,
'O fair maid, would ye that sodger ken?' —
'In troth I't well an that I wad,
Amang ten thousand men.'
Te dilly etc.

'O fair maid, what if I be the man,
O fair maid what if I be the man?' —
'In troth I't well it may be sae,
I'se had ye for the same.'
Te dilly dan, etc.

whase aught – whose property; *bairn* – child; *sodger's* – soldier's; *spear* – ask; *mair*
– more; *hame* – home; *ken* – know; *I't* – I know it; *an* – whether; *wad* – would; *sae*
– so; *I'se had* – I shall take.

119   Let me in this ae Night

O Lassie, art thou sleeping yet,
Or art thou wakin, I would wit?
For Love has bound me hand and foot,
    And I would fain be in, jo.

            Chorus
    O let me in this ae night,
    This ae, ae, ae night;
    For pity's sake this ae night,
    O rise and let me in, jo.

Thou hear'st the winter wind an weet;
Nae star blinks thro' the driving sleet;
Take pity on my weary feet,
    And shield me frae the rain, jo.
        O let me in, etc.

The bitter blast that round me blaws,
Unheeded howls, unheeded fa's;
The cauldness o' thy heart's the cause
    Of a' my grief and pine, jo.
        O let me in, etc.

Her Answer

O tell na me o' wind and rain,
Upbraid na me wi' cauld disdain,
Gae back the gate ye cam again,
   I winna let ye in, jo.

Chorus
I tell you now this ae night,
This ae, ae, ae night;
And ance for a' this ae night,
I winna let ye in, jo.

The snellest blast, at mirkest hours,
That round the pathless wanderer pours
Is nocht to what poor She endures,
   That's trusted faithless Man, jo.
    I tell you now, etc.

The sweetest flower that deck'd the mead,
Now trodden like the vilest weed —
Let simple maid the lesson read,
   The weird may be her ain, jo.
    I tell you now, etc.

The bird that charm'd his summer day,
And now the cruel Fowler's prey;
Let that to witless woman say
   The gratefu' heart of man, jo.
    I tell you now, etc.

Robert Burns

wit – know; *jo* – sweetheart; *ae* – one; *weet* – wet; *frae* – from; *fa's* – falls; *pine* – sorrow; *na* – not; *gate* – way; *winna* – won't; *ance* – once; *snellest* – keenest; *mirkest* – darkest; *nocht* – nothing; *weird* – fate; *ain* – own.

DIALOGUES

120   Will ye go to the Ew-Buchts, Marion?

Will ye go to the ew-buchts, Marion,
    And wear in the sheep wi' me?
The sun shines sweet, my Marion,
    But nae half so sweet as thee.
O Marion's a bonny lass,
    And the blyth blink's in her eye:
And fain wad I marry Marion,
    Gin Marion wad marry me.

There's gowd in your garters, Marion,
    And silk on your white hauss-bane;
Fu' fain wad I kiss my Marion,
    At e'en, when I come hame.
There's braw lads in Earnslaw, Marion,
    Wha gape, and glower wi' their eye,
At kirk when they see my Marion;
    But nane o' them lo'es like me.

I've nine milk-ews, my Marion,
    A cow and a brawny quey;
I'll gi'e them a' to my Marion,
    Just on her bridal day.
And ye's get a green sey apron,
    And waistcoat of the London brown;
And wow but ye will be vap'ring
    Whene'er ye gang to the town.

I'm young and stout, my Marion;
    Nane dances like me on the green:
And gin ye forsake me, Marion,
    I'll e'en gae draw up wi' Jean:
Sae put on your pearlins, Marion,
    And kyrtle of the cramasie;
And soon as my chin has nae hair on,
    I shall come west, and see ye.

— pens in which ewes were milked; *wear* — drive to the fold with caution; *nae* — not; *blink* — glance; *gin* — if; *gowd* — gold; *hauss-bane* — collar-bone; *fu'* — full; *wad* — would; *hame* — home; *braw* — fine; *glower* — stare; *kirk* — church; *nane* — none; *brawny* — streaked with black and brown; *quey* — young cow of about two years; *sey* — home-made woollen cloth; *vap'ring* — boasting; *gang* — go; *gin* — if; *draw up wi'* — start courting; *pearlins* — laces made of thread or silk; *cramasie* — crimson.

121   The yellow hair'd Laddie

The yellow hair'd laddie sat down on yon brae,
Cries, 'Milk the ews, lassie, let nane of them gae';
And ay she milked, and ay she sang,
The yellow hair'd laddie shall be my goodman.
And ay she milked, etc.

'The weather is cauld, and my claithing is thin;
The ews are new clipped, they winna bught in:
They winna bught in tho' I should die,
O yellow hair'd laddie, be kind to me.'
They winna bught in, etc.

The goodwife cries butt the house, 'Jenny, come ben,
The cheese is to mak, and the butter's to kirn.' —
'Tho' butter, and cheese, and a' shou'd sour,
I'll crack and kiss wi' my love ae haff-hour;
It's ae haff-hour, and we's e'en mak it three,
For the yellow hair'd laddie my husband shall be.'

brae — hill; *nane* — none; *gae* — go; *goodman* — husband; *cauld* — cold; *claithing* — clothing; *winna* — won't; *bught* — fold; *goodwife* — mistress of the house; *butt* — towards the outer room of the house; *ben* — inside; *kirn* — churn; *a'* — all; *crack* — chat; *ae* — one; *we'se e'en* — we'll just.

122   My Peggy is a Young Thing

My Peggy is a young thing,
    Just enter'd in her teens,
Fair as the day, and sweet as May,
Fair as the day, and always gay:
    My Peggy is a young thing,
        And I'm not very auld,
    Yet weel I like to meet her at
        The wauking o' the fauld.

My Peggy speaks sae sweetly
   Whene'er we meet alane,
I wish nae mair to lay my care,
I wish nae mair o' a' that's rare:
   My Peggy speaks sae sweetly,
      To a' the lave I'm cauld;
   But she gars a' my spirits glow,
      At wauking o' the fauld.

My Peggy smiles sae kindly
   Whene'er I whisper love,
That I look down on a' the town,
That I look down upon a crown.
   My Peggy smiles sae kindly,
      It makes me blythe and bauld,
   And naething gi'es me sic delight,
      As wauking o' the fauld.

My Peggy sings sae saftly,
   When on my pipe I play;
By a' the rest it is confest,
By a' the rest that she sings best.
   My Peggy sings sae saftly,
      And in her sangs are tald,
   Wi' innocence the wale o' sense,
      At wauking o' the fauld.

Allan Ramsay

auld – old; *wauking* – watching; *fauld* – fold; *nae mair* – no more; *a'* – all; *sae* – so;
lave – rest; *gars* – makes; *bauld* – bold; *wale* – choice, pick.

123   The Bob of Dumblane

Lassie, lend me your braw hemp heckle,
   And I'll lend you my thripling kame;
For fainness, deary, I'll gar ye keckle,
   If ye'll go dance the *Bob of Dumblane.*

Haste ye, gang to the ground of your trunkies,
   Busk ye braw, and dinna think shame;
Consider in time, if leading of monkies
   Be better than dancing the *Bob of Dumblane.*

Be frank, my lassie, lest I grow fickle,
   And take my word and offer again.
Syne ye may chance to repent it mickle,
   Ye did nae accept of the *Bob of Dumblane.*
The dinner, the piper, and priest shall be ready,
   And I'm grown dowy with lying my lane;
Away then, leave baith minny and dady,
   And try with me the *Bob of Dumblane.*

Allan Ramsay

Bob of Dumblane — name of dance, with equivocal meaning; *braw* — fine; *heckle* — comb for splitting fibres; *thripling kame* — comb-like implement for splitting flax or hemp; *fainness* — pleasure; *gar* — make; *keckle* — laugh immoderately; *gang* — go; *ground* — bottom; *trunkies* — clothes-chests; *busk ye braw* — dress finely; *leading of monkies* — after death, old maids were supposed to lead apes in Hell; *syne* — then; *mickle* — much; *dowy* — doleful; *my lane* — alone; *minny* — mother.

124   The Lee Rigg

Will ye gang o'er the lee-rigg,
   My ain kind deary O!
And cuddle there sae kindly
   Wi' me, my kind deary O?

At thornie-dike and birken-tree
   We'll daff, and ne'er be weary, O;
They'll scug ill een frae you and me,
   Mine ain kind deary O.

Nae herds wi' kent or colly there,
   Shall ever come to fear ye O;
But lav'rocks, whistling in the air,
   Shall woo, like me, their deary O!

              PASTORAL

While others herd their lambs and ewes,
    And toil for warld's gear, my jo,
Upon the lee my pleasure grows,
    Wi' you, my kind deary O!

Robert Fergusson

gang — go; *lee-rigg* — meadow ridge; *ain* — own; *thornie-dike* — hawthorn hedge; *birken* — birch; *daff* — dally; *scug* — screen; *e'en* — eyes; *herd* — shepherd; *kent* — pole used for leaping ditches; *lav'rocks* — larks; *jo* — sweetheart.

125   Ca' the Yowes

Chorus
Ca' the yowes to the knowes,
    Ca' them whare the heather grows,
Ca' them whare the burnie rowes,
    My bonie Dearie.

Hark, the mavis' evening sang
Sounding Clouden's woods amang;
Then a faulding let us gang,
    My bonie Dearie.
        Ca' the yowes, etc.

We'll gae down by Clouden side,
Thro' the hazels spreading-wide
O'er the waves, that sweetly glide
    To the moon sae clearly.
        Ca' the yowes, etc.

Yonder Clouden's silent towers,
Where at moonshine midnight hours
O'er the dewy bending flowers
    Fairies dance sae cheary.
        Ca' the yowes, etc.

Ghaist nor bogle shalt thou fear,
Thou'rt to Love and Heav'n sae dear,
Nocht of Ill may come thee near;
    My bonie Dearie.
        Ca' the yowes, etc.

Fair and lovely as thou art,
Thou hast stown my very heart;
I can die — but canna part,
    My bonnie Dearie.
        Ca' the yowes, etc.

Robert Burns

ca' — drive; *yowes* — ewes; *knowes* — knolls; *burnie* — streamlet; *rowes* — rolls; *mavis* — thrush; *Clouden* — tributary of the Nith, in Dumfriesshire; *a faulding* — folding; *gang* — go; *silent towers* — of Lincluden Abbey; *ghaist* — ghost; *bogle* — goblin; *stown* — stolen; *canna* — cannot.

126   Corn Rigs

It was upon a Lammas night,
    When corn rigs are bonie,
Beneath the moon's unclouded light,
    I held awa to Annie:
The time flew by, wi' tentless heed,
    Till 'tween the late and early;
Wi' sma' persuasion she agreed,
    To see me thro' the barley.

            Chorus
    Corn rigs, an' barley rigs,
        An' corn rigs are bonie:
    I'll ne'er forget that happy night,
        Amang the rigs wi' Annie.

The sky was blue, the wind was still,
    The moon was shining clearly;
I set her down, wi' right good will,
    Amang the rigs o' barley:
I kent her heart was a' my ain;
    I lov'd her most sincerely;
I kiss'd her owre and owre again,
    Amang the rigs o' barley.
        Corn rigs, an' barley rigs, etc.

I lock'd her in my fond embrace;
    Her heart was beating rarely:
My blessings on that happy place,
    Amang the rigs o' barley!
But by the moon and stars so bright,
    That shone that hour so clearly!
She ay shall bless that happy night
    Amang the rigs o' barley.
        Corn rigs, an' barley rigs, etc.

I hae been blythe wi' Comrades dear;
    I hae been merry drinking:
I hae been joyfu' gath'rin gear;
    I hae been happy thinking:
But a' the pleasures e'er I saw,
    Tho' three times doubl'd fairly,
That happy night was worth them a',
    Amang the rigs o' barley.
        Corn rigs, an' barley rigs, etc.

Robert Burns

Lammas − 1 August, the time of harvest; *rigs* − ridges; *awa* − away; *tentless heed* −
careless regard; *late and early* − dark and dawn; *kent* − knew; *owre* − over; *ay* −
always; *gath'rin gear* − money-making.

127   Ettrick Banks

On Ettrick banks, in a summer's night,
    At glowming, when the sheep drave hame,
I met my lassie braw and tight,
    Come wading barefoot a' her lane.
My heart grew light — I ran, I flang
    My arms about her lilly neck,
And kiss'd and clapp'd her there fu' lang,
    My words they were na mony, feck.

I said, 'My lassie, will ye go
    To the Highland hills, the Earse to learn?
I'll baith gi'e thee a cow and ew,
    When ye come to the brigg of Earn:
At Leith, auld meal comes in, ne'er fash,
    And herrings at the Broomy Law;
Chear up your heart, my bonny lass,
    There's gear to win we never saw.

All day when we have wrought enough,
    When winter's frost and snaw begin,
And when the sun gaes west the loch,
    At night when you sit down to spin,
I'll screw my pipes and play a spring:
    And thus the weary night we'll end,
Till the tender kid and lamb-time bring
    Our pleasant summer back again.

Syne when the trees are in their bloom,
    And gowans glent o'er ilka field,
I'll meet my lass amang the broom,
    And lead you to my summer shield.
Then far frae a' their scornfu' din,
    That make the kindly hearts their sport,
We'll laugh, and kiss, and dance, and sing,
    And gar the langest day seem short.'

Ettrick — river in Selkirkshire; *hame* — home; *braw and tight* — in her finery, and looking neat; *her lane* — alone; *clapp'd* — embraced; *mony* — many; *feck* — in faith; *Earse* — Gaelic; *baith* — both; *Earn* — tributary of River Tay in Perthshire; *auld* — old; *fash* — trouble; *Broomy Law* — quay on River Clyde, Glasgow; *gaes west* — goes west (of); *spring* — lively tune; *syne* — then; *gowans* — daisies; *glent* — glint; *shield* — hut for herdsmen; *frae* — from; *gar* — make. *Note* — ·the last stanza was added in *Tea-Table Miscellany*, vol. IV (1733), and presumably is by Allan Ramsay himself.

128   My Love was born in Aberdeen

My love was born in Aberdeen,
The boniest lad that e'er was seen,
O he is forced frae me to gae
O'er the hills and far away!

> *Chorus*
> *O he's a ranting, roving laddie!*
> *O he's a brisk and bonie laddie!*
> *Betide what will, I'll get me ready*
> *And follow the lad wi' the Highland plaidie.*

I'll sell my rock, my reel, my tow,
My gude gray mare and hacket cow,
To buy my love a tartan plaid,
Because he is a roving blade.
> *O he's a ranting, roving laddie, etc.*

gae -- go; *rock* — distaff; *tow* — thread; *hacket* — white-faced.

129   Liza Baillie

'My bonny Liza Baillie,
    I'll row you in my plaidy,
If you will gang alang wi' me
    And be a Highland lady.'

'If I wad gang alang wi' you,
    They wadna ca' me wise, Sir,
For I can neither card nor spin,
    Nor yet can I speak Erse, Sir.'

HIGHLAND AND LOWLAND

'My bonny Liza Baillie,
    Your minny canna want you;
Sae let the trooper gang his lane
    And carry his ain portmanteau.'

But she's cast aff her bonny shoon,
    Made of the Spanish leather,
And she's put on her Highland brogues
    To skip amang the heather.

And she's cast aff her bonny gown
    A' wrought wi' gowd and satin,
And she's put on a tartan plaid
    To sport amang the brachen.

She wadna' ha'e a Lawland laird
    Nor be an English lady:
But she's awa' wi' Duncan Grahame,
    He's row'd her in his plaidy.

row — roll; *gang* — go; *wad* — would; *Erse* — Gaelic; *minny* — mother; *his lane* —
alone; *gowd* — gold; *ha'e* — have.

'Where ha'e ye been a' day,
Bonny Laddie, Highland Laddie?' —
'Up the bank and down the brae
Seeking Maggie, seeking Maggie.'

'Where ha'e ye been a' day,
Bonny Laddie, Highland Laddie?' —
'Down the back o' Bell's Wynd,
Courting Maggie, courting Maggie.'

ha'e — have; *brae* — hill; *Bell's Wynd* — a lane to the south of the High Street,
Edinburgh.

Donald Brodie met a lass,
   Comin' o'er the hills o' Coupar,
Donald wi' his Highland hand
   Graipit a' the bits about her.

     Chorus
Comin' o'er the hills o' Coupar,
Comin' o'er the hills o' Coupar,
Donald in a sudden wrath
He ran his Highland durk into her.

Weel I wat she was a quine,
   Wad made a body's mouth to water;
Our Mess John, wi's auld grey pow,
   His haly lips wad licket at her.
Comin' o'er the hills, etc.

Up she started in a fright,
   Thro' the braes what she could bicker:
Let her gang, quo' Donald, now,
   For in him's nerse my shot is sicker.
Comin' o'er the hills, etc.

                            Robert Burns

Coupar – i.e. near Coupar Angus; *graipit* – felt; *durk* – dirk, *sc.* penis; *wat* – know; *wad* – would have; *Mess John* – parish minister; *auld* – old; *haly* – holy; *braes* – hills; *bicker* – hurry; *gang* – go; *him's nerse* – her arse; *sicker* – secure.

132   Had I the Wyte

Had I the wyte, had I the wyte,
   Had I the wyte she bad me;
For she was steward in the house,
   And I was fit-man laddie;
And when I wadna do't again,
   A silly cow she ca'd me;
She straik't my head, and clapt my cheeks,
   And lous'd my breeks and bad me.

Could I for shame, could I for shame,
    Could I for shame deny her;
Or in the bed was I to blame,
    She bad me lye beside her:
I pat six inches in her wame,
    A quarter wadna fly'd her;
For ay the mair I ca'd it hame,
    Her ports they grew the wider.

My tartan plaid, when it was dark,
    Could I refuse to share it;
She lifted up her holland-sark,
    And bad me fin' the gair o't:
Or how could I amang the garse,
    But gie her hilt and hair o't;
She clasped her houghs about my arse,
    And ay she glowr'd for mair o't.

? Robert Burns

wyte – shame; *fit-man* – footman; *wadna* – wouldn't; *straik't* – stroked; *lous'd my breeks* – loosened my breeches; *pat* – put; *wame* – belly; *quarter* – of a yard; *fly'd* – frightened; *mair* – more; *ca'd* – drove; *holland-sark* – linen shift; *gair* – crease; *garse* – grass; *glowr'd* – stared. (Burns probably had a hand in this variant of a traditional bawdy song.)

133   Charlie, he's my Darling

'Twas on a Monday morning,
    Right early in the year,
That Charlie cam to our town,
    The young Chevalier.

   Chorus
An' Charlie, he's my darling,
My darling, my darling,
Charlie, he's my darling,
    The young Chevalier.

As he was walking up the street,
    The city for to view,
O there he spied a bonie lass
    The window looking thro',
An' Charlie, etc.

Sae light's he jimped up the stair,
    And tirled at the pin;
And wha sae ready as hersel
    To let the laddie in.
An' Charlie, etc.

He set his Jenny on his knee,
    All in his Highland dress;
For brawlie weel he ken'd the way
    To please a bonie lass.
An' Charlie, etc.

It's up yon hethery mountain,
    And down yon scroggie glen,
We daur na gang a milking,
    For Charlie and his men.
An' Charlie, etc.

                                        Robert Burns

tirl'd – rattled; *pin* – door-latch; *sae* – so; *brawlie* – bravely; *scroggie* – covered with
stunted bushes; *daur na gang* – dare not go.

134   The Cock Laird

A Cock laird fou cadgie,
    With Jenny did meet,
He haws'd her, he kiss'd her,
    And ca'd her his sweet.
'Wilt thou gae alang
    Wi' me, Jenny, Jenny?
Thouse be my ain lemman,
    Jo Jenny,' quoth he.

'If I gae alang wi' ye,
    Ye maunna fail
To feast me with caddels
    And good hacket kail.'
'The deil's in your nicety,
    Jenny,' quoth he,
'Mayna bannocks of bear-meal
    Be as good for thee?'

'And I maun hae pinners,
    With pearling set round,
A skirt of puddy,
    And a waistcoat of brown.'
'Awa' with sic vanities,
    Jenny,' quoth he,
'For kurchis and kirtles
    Are fitter for thee.

My lairdship can yield me
    As meikle a year,
As had us in pottage
    And good knockit bear:
But having nae tenants,
    O Jenny, Jenny,
To buy ought I ne'er have
    A penny,' quoth he.

'The borrowstoun merchants
  Will sell ye on tick,
For we maun hae braw things,
  Albeit they soud break.
When broken, frae care
  The fools are set free,
When we make them lairds
  In the Abbey,' quoth she.

Allan Ramsay

Cock laird — landholder who cultivates his own estate; *fou cadgie* — very sportive; *hàws'd* — embraced; *gae* — go; *thouse* — you shall; *Jo* — dear; *maunna* — must not; *caddels* — spiced drinks; *hacket-kail* — chopped colewort; *deil* — devil; *bannocks* — cakes; *bear* — barley; *pinners* — headgear with lappets pinned to the temples, reaching down to the breast and fastened there; *pearling* — lace; *kurchis* — kerchiefs; *lairdship* — estate; *meikle* — much; *knockit bear* — barley stripped of husks 'by beating in a hollow stone with a maul' (Jamieson); *borrowstoun* — royal burgh; *tick* — credit; *braw* — fine; *soud break* — should go bankrupt; *lairds in the Abbey* — bankrupts, who could seek sanctuary in Holyrood Abbey, Edinburgh.

135   The Three Nuns in the Cowgate

There's a land in the Cowgate that's kept by lasses,
It may be weel kent by ilk ane that passes;
They will rather take fiddlers, pipers, and drums,
Before that they'll stand by the name of the Nuns.

> *Chorus*
> *An auld maid and a hantle o' siller,*
> *An auld maid and a hantle o' siller;*
> *Gin she hadna haen that, fient ane wad gane till her;*
> *An auld maid and a hantle o' siller.*

The first that gaed aff was Mistress Ann,
Who vow'd and declar'd that she'd ha'e a man;
She wad ha'e a man, and she'd tarry nae langer,
For at the Nun's Land she had tane a great anger.
  An auld maid, etc.

The next that gaed aff was Mistress Mary,
Who vow'd and declar'd that she wad miscarry;
And if she miscarry'd she was surely undone,
For she mortally hated the name of a Nun.
    An auld maid, etc.

Now good Mistress Jean is left all alone,
To sigh and to sob, and make great moan;
Will nae body come and tak pity on me
And marry me quickly before that I die?
    Some auld women gang mad for to marry,
    Some auld women gang mad for to marry;
    In the shape of a man they wou'd jump at Auld Harry;
    Some auld women gang mad for to marry.

Cowgate – to the south of High Street, in Edinburgh, between the Grassmarket and Holyrood Road; *Land* – house of several stories, including different tenements; *weel kent* – well known; *ilk ane* – each one; *hantle* – large sum; *siller* – money; *gin* – if; *haen* – had; *fient ane* – devil a one; *wad gane till* – would have gone to; *nae langer* – no longer; *miscarry* – go to the bad; *gang* – go; *Auld Harry* – the devil.

136   Heh how, Johny Lad

Heh how, Johny lad, ye're no sae kind's
    ye sud hae been,
Heh how, Johny lad, ye're no sae kind's
    ye sud hae been,
Sae weel's ye might hae touzled me and
    sweetly pried my mow bedeen –
Heh how, etc.

My father he was at the pleugh, my mither
    she was at the mill,
My billie he was at the moss, and no ane
    near our sport to spill,
The fint a body was therein, ye need na
    fley'd for being seen:
Heh how, etc.

But I man hae anither jo wha's love gangs
    never out o' mind,
And winna let the mamens pass when to
    a lass he can be kind:
Then gang yere ways to blinking Bess,
    nae mair for Johny sal she green,
Heh how, Johny lad, ye're no sae kind's
    ye sud hae been.

sud – should; *hae* – have; *pried* – tasted; *mow* – mouth; *bedeen* – again and again;
pleugh – plough; *billie* – brother; *the fint a body* – devil a person; *need na fley'd
for* – need not have been afraid of; *man* – must; *jo* – sweetheart; *blinking* – ogling;
sal – shall; *green* – pine.

137   Duncan Gray

Can ye play me Duncan Gray,
    Ha, ha, the girdin' o't;
O'er the hills an' far awa,
    Ha, ha, ha, the girdin' o't,
Duncan came our Meg to woo,
Meg was nice an' wadna do,
But like an ither puff'd an' blew
    At offer o' the girdin' o't.

Duncan, he cam here again,
    Ha, ha, the girdin' o't,
A' was out, an' Meg her lane,
    Ha, ha, ha, the girdin' o't;
He kiss'd her butt, he kiss'd her ben,
He bang'd a thing against her wame;
But, troth, I now forget its name,
    But, I trow, she gat the girdin' o't.

 She took him to the cellar then,
    Ha, ha, the girdin' o't,
To see gif he could do't again,
    Ha, ha, ha, the girdin' o't;
He kiss'd her ance, he kiss'd her twice,
An' by the bye he kiss'd her thrice
Till deil a mair the thing wad rise
    To gie her the long girdin' o't.

But Duncan took her to his wife,
   Ha, ha, the girdin' o't,
To be the comfort o' his life,
   Ha, ha, ha, the girdin' o't;
An' now she scauls baith night an' day,
Except when Duncan's at the play;
An' that's as seldom as he may,
   He's weary o' the girdin' o't.

girdin' — striking (euphemism); *nice* — fastidious; *ither* — adder; *her lane* — alone; *butt* — in the outer room; *ben* — in the inner room; *wame* — belly; *gif* — if; *deil a mair* — devil the more; *scauls* — scolds; *the play* — sexual intercourse.
(Burns probably had a hand in tidying up this piece. There is an earlier version, with an additional stanza, in the Herd MS.)

138   Duncan Gray

Weary fa' you, Duncan Gray,
   Ha, ha the girdin o't,
Wae gae by you, Duncan Gray,
   Ha, ha the girdin o't;
When a' the lave gae to their play,
Then I maun sit the lee-lang day,
And jeeg the cradle wi' my tae
   And a' for the bad girdin o't.

Bonie was the lammas moon,
   Ha, ha the girdin o't,
Glowrin a' the hills aboon,
   Ha, ha the girdin o't,
The girdin brak, the beast cam down,
I tint my curch and baith my shoon,
And Duncan ye're an unco loon;
   Wae on the bad girdin o't.

But Duncan gin ye'll keep your aith,
   Ha, ha the girdin.o't,
I'se bless you wi' my hindmost breath,
   Ha, ha the girdin o't,

Duncan gin ye'll keep your aith,
The beast again can bear us baith,
And auld Mess John will mend the skaith
  And clout the bad girdin o't.

Robert Burns

Weary fa' – woe befall; *girdin* – girthing (with secondary sense as in 137); *wae gae by* – woe go with; *a' the lave* – all the rest; *maun* – must; *lee-lang* – live-long; *jeeg* – jog; *tae* – toe; *lammas* – harvest; *glowrin* – staring; *aboon* – above; *tint* – lost; *curch* – kerchief; *shoon* – shoes; *unco loon* – terrible rogue; *gin* – if; *aith* – oath; *I'se* – I shall; *Mess John* – parish minister; *skaith* – damage; *clout* – patch.

139   Last May a braw Wooer

Last May a braw wooer cam down the lang glen,
  And sair wi' his love he did deave me;
I said, there was naething I hated like men –
  The deuce gae wi'm, to believe me, believe me;
  The deuce gae wi'm, to believe me.

He spak o' the darts in my bonie black een,
  And vow'd for my love he was dying;
I said, he might die when he liked for Jean –
  The Lord forgie me for lying, for lying,
  The Lord forgie me for lying!

A weel-stocked mailen, himsel' for the laird,
  And marriage aff-hand, were his proffers;
I never loot on that I kend it, or car'd;
  But thought I might hae waur offers, waur offers;
  But thought I might hae waur offers.

But what wad ye think? – in a fortnight or less,
  The deil tak his taste to gae near her!
He up the lang loan to my black cousin, Bess,
  Guess ye how, the jad! I could bear her, could bear her;
  Guess ye how, the jad! I could bear her.

But a' the niest week as I petted wi' care,
  I gaed to the tryste o' Dalgarnock;
And wha but my fine fickle lover was there,
  I glowr'd as I'd seen a warlock, a warlock,
  I glowr'd as I'd seen a warlock.

But owre my left shouther I gae him a blink,
  Lest neebours might say I was saucy:
My wooer he caper'd as he'd been in drink,
  And vow'd I was his dear lassie, dear lassie,
  And vow'd I was his dear lassie.

I spier'd for my cousin fu' couthy and sweet,
  Gin she had recover'd her hearin,
And how her new shoon fit her auld shachl't feet;
  But, heavens! how he fell a swearin, a swearin,
  But, heavens! how he fell a swearin.

He begged, for Gudesake, I wad be his wife,
  Or else I wad kill him wi' sorrow:
So e'en to preserve the poor body in life,
  I think I maun wed him to-morrow, to-morrow,
  I think I maun wed him to-morrow.

Robert Burns

braw — fine; *lang* — long; *sair* — sorely; *deave* — deafen; *gae* — go; *een* — eyes;
weel-stocked mailen — well stocked farm; *laird* — landlord; *aff-hand* — off hand; *loot*
— let; *kend* — knew; *waur* — worse; *wad* — would; *deil* — devil; *loan* — strip of grass
running through arable ground; *jad* — jade; *niest* — next; *tryste* — cattle fair;
Dalgarnock — on River Nith in Dumfriesshire; *glowr'd* — stared; *warlock* — wizard;
owre — over; *sh'outher* — shoulder; *blink* — glance; *spier'd* — asked; *couthy* — kindly;
gin — if; *shachl't* — shapeless; *maun* — must.

140   Woo'd and Married and a'

Wooed and married and a',
    Married and wooed and a';
The dandilly toast of the parish
    Is wooed and married and a'.
The wooers will now ride thinner,
    And by, when they wonted to ca';
'Tis needless to speer for the lassie
    That's wooed and married and a'.

The girss had na freedom of growing
    As lang as she wasna awa',
Nor in the town could there be stowing
    For wooers that wanted to ca'.
For drinking and dancing and brulyies,
    And boxing and shaking of fa's,
The town was for ever in tulyies;
    But now the lassie's awa'.

But had they but ken'd her as I did,
    Their errand it wad ha'e been sma';
She neither kent spinning nor carding,
    Nor brewing nor baking ava'.
But wooers ran all mad upon her,
    Because she was bonnie and braw,
And sae I dread will be seen on her,
    When she's byhand and awa'.

He'll roose her but sma' that has married her,
    Now when he's gotten her a',
And wish, I fear, he had miscarry'd her,
    Tocher and ribbons and a'.
For her art it lay all in her dressing;
    But gin her braws ance were awa',
I fear she'll turn out o' the fashion,
    And knit up her moggans with straw.

For yesterday I yeed to see her,
    And O she was wonderous braw,
Yet she cried to her husband to gie her
    An ell of red ribbons or twa.
He up and he set doun beside her
    A reel and a wheelie to ca';
She said, Was he this gate to guide her?
    And out at the door and awa'.

Her neist road was hame till her mither,
    Who speer'd at her now, How was a'?
She says till her, 'Was't for nae ither
    That I was married awa'.
But gae and sit down to a wheelie,
    And at it baith night and day ca',
As ha'e the yarn reeled by a cheelie,
    That ever was crying to draw?'

Her mother says till her, 'Hech, lassie,
    He's wisest, I fear, of the twa;
Ye'll ha'e little to put in the bassie,
    Gin ye be backward to draw.
'Tis now ye should work like a tiger
    And at it baith wallop and ca',
As lang's ye ha'e youthhead and vigour,
    And little anes and debt are awa'.

'Sae swythe awa' hame to your hadding,
    Mair fool than when ye came awa';
Ye maunna now keep ilka wedding,
    Nor gae sae clean-fingered and braw;
But mind with a neiper you're yokit,
    And that ye your end o't maun draw,
Or else ye deserve to be dockit;
    Sae that is an answer for a'.'

Young lucky now finds herself nidder'd,
    And wist na well what gate to ca';
But with hersel even considered
    That hamewith were better to draw,

                THE MARRIAGE YOKE

And e'en tak her chance of her landing,
    However the matter might fa';
Folk need not on frets to be standing
    That's wooed and married and a'.

Alexander Ross

dandilly – overpraised (for beauty); *by* – past; *wonted* – were accustomed to; *speer* – ask; *girss* – grass; *brulyies* – broils; *shaking of fa's* – wrestling; *tulyies* – turmoils; *ava'* – at all; *byhand* – out of the way; *roose* – praise; *but sma'* – scantily; *miscarry'd* – failed in his courtship of her; *tocher* – dowry; *braws* – fine clothes; *moggans* – footless stockings; *yeed* – went; *ca'* – drive, wind; *gate* – way, manner; *neist* – next; *till* – to; *cheelie* – fellow; *draw* – pull (of thread), spin; *bassie* – wooden dish in which meal for immediate use was kept; *swythe* – quickly; *hadding* – house and household goods; *mauna* – must not; *keep* – celebrate; *ilka* – every; *neiper* – neighbour; *dockit* – spanked; *lucky* – housewife; *nidder'd* – put down; *hamewith* – homewards; *frets* – petty irritations. (A highly wrought *genre* song that takes off from an older original, one version of which is printed in Herd's *Scottish Song,* 1776, although in all probability it goes back to the early years of the century.)

141   The Husband's Complaint

If ever there was an ill wife i' the warld,
It was my hap to get her,
And by my hap and by my luck:
I had been better but her.

I wish I had been laid i' my grave,
When I got her to marriage,
For the very first night the strife began,
And she gave me my carriage.

I scour'd awa to Edinborow-town
And my cutty brown together,
And there I bought her a braw new gown:
I'm sure it cost some siller.

Ilka ell o't was a crown,
'T was better than her marriage,
But because it was black, an' it was na brown,
For that I got my carriage.

When I saw naething her wad mend,
I took her to the forest,
The very first wood that I came to,
Green-holan was the nearest.

There I paid her baith back and side,
Till a' her banes play'd clatter,
And a' the bairns gather'd round about,
Cry'd: 'Fy, goodman, have at her!'

hap – lot; *but* – without; *carriage* – tongue-lashing; *scour'd* – rode hard; *cutty brown* – dock-tailed brown horse; *braw* – fine; *siller* – cash; *ilka* – each; *was* – i.e. cost; *wad* – would; *holan* – holly; *baith* – both.

142   Fairly shot of her

I married a wife with a good commendation
But now she's as peeck to a' the whole nation;
Hearken and hear, and I will tell ye a note of her,
Now she is dead, and I'm fairly shot of her.

Chorus
Fairly, fairly, fairly shot of her,
Now she is dead I will dance on the top of her,
Well's me now I am fairly shot of her,
Fairly, etc.

peeck – notorious; *a'* – all; *shot* – rid.

143   O that I had ne'er been married

O that I had ne'er been married,
I wad never had nae care,
Now I've gotten wife and bairns
They cry 'crowdie' evermair.

Chorus
Ance crowdie, twice crowdie,
Three times crowdie in a day:
Gin ye crowdie ony may
Ye'll crowdie a' my meal away!

crowdie — thick oatmeal gruel; *ance* — once; *gin* — if; *ony may* — any more.

144   The Ducks dang o'er my Daddie

The nine-pint Bicker's faen aff the Binck,
    And broken the ten pint Cannie.
The wife and her cummers sat down to drink,
    But ne'er a drap gae the Goodmanie, O.

The bairns they set up the cry,
    'The Ducks hae dang o'er my Daddy.'
'There's no muckle matter,' quo' the Goodwife,
    'For he was but a daidling bodie.'

dang o'er — beaten down; *Bicker* — beaker; *faen aff* — fallen off; *Binck* — dresser;
cummers — gossips; *Goodmanie* — husband; *bairns* — children; *daidling* — doddering.

145   Wad ye do That?

'Gudewife, when your gudeman's frae hame,
    Might I but be sae bauld,
As come to your bed-chamber,
    When winter nights are cauld;
As come to your bed-chamber,
    When nights are cauld and wat,
And lie in your gudeman's stead,
    Wad ye do that?'

THE MARRIAGE YOKE   145

'Young man, an ye should be so kind,
    When our gudeman's frae hame,
As come to my bed-chamber,
    Where I am laid my lane;
And lie in our gudeman's stead,
    I will tell you what,
He fucks me five times ilka night,
    Wad ye do that?'

wad − would; *gudewife* − mistress of the house; *gudeman* − husband; *wat* − wet; *laid my lane* − lying alone; *ilka* − every.

146   Sic a Wife as Willie's Wife

Willie Wastle dwalls on Tweed,
    The spot they ca' it Linkumdoddie;
A creeshie wabster till his trade,
    Can steal a clue wi' ony body:
He has a wife that's dour and din,
    Tinkler Madgie was her mither;
Sic a wife as Willie's wife,
    I wad na gie a button for her.

She has an e'e, she has but ane,
    Our cat has twa, the very colour;
Five rusty teeth, forbye a stump,
    A clapper-tongue wad deave a miller:
A whiskin beard about her mou,
    Her nose and chin they threaten ither;
Sic a wife as Willie's wife,
    I wad na gie a button for her.

She's bow-hough'd, she's hem-shin'd,
    Ae limpin leg a hand-bread shorter;
She's twisted right, she's twisted left,
    To balance fair in ilka quarter:
She has a hump upon her breast,
    The twin o' that upon her shouther;
Sic a wife as Willie's wife,
    I wad na gie a button for her.

THE MARRIAGE YOKE

Auld baudrans by the ingle sits,
    An wi' her loof her face a washin;
But Willie's wife is nae sae trig,
    She dights her grunzie wi' a hushian:
Her waly nieves like midden-creels,
    Her feet wad fyle the Logan-water;
Sic a wife as Willie's wife,
    I wad na gie a button for her.

Robert Burns

dwalls – dwells; *ca'* – call; *creeshie wabster* – filthy weaver; *till* – to; *clue* – ball of thread or yarn; *dour* – hard; *din* – muddy complexioned; *tinkler* – tinker; *sic* – such; *wad na gie* – would not give; *e'e* – eye; *ane* – one; *forbye* – in addition to; *deave* – deafen; *mou* – mouth; *ither* – each other (i.e. they almost meet); *bow-hough'd* – bandy-legged; *hem-shin'd* – 'with shins shaped like *haims,* the curved pieces of wood or metal fixed over a draught-horse's collar' (Kinsley); *ae* – one; *hand-bread* – hand's breadth; *ilka* – either; *shouther* – shoulder; *baudrans* – the cat; *ingle* – fireside; *loof* – paw; *nae sae trig* – not so fastidious; *dights her grunzie* – wipes her snout; *hushian* – footless stocking; *waly nieves* – ample fists; *midden-creels* – manure baskets; *fyle* – foul; *Logan* – tributary of the Tweed.

147   My Spouse Nancy

'Husband, husband, cease your strife,
    Nor longer idly rave, Sir;
Tho' I am your wedded wife,
    Yet I am not your slave, Sir.'

'One of two must still obey,
    Nancy, Nancy;
Is it Man or Woman, say,
    My spouse Nancy?'

'If 'tis still the lordly word,
    Service and obedience,
I'll desert my Sov'reign lord,
    And so, goodbye, Allegiance!'

'Sad will I be, so bereft,
    Nancy, Nancy;
Yet I'll try to make a shift,
    My spouse Nancy.'

'My poor heart, then break it must,
    My last hour I am near it:
When you lay me in the dust,
    Think how you will bear it.'

'I will hope and trust in Heaven,
    Nancy, Nancy;
Strength to bear it will be given,
    My spouse Nancy.'

'Well, Sir, from the silent dead,
    Still I'll try to daunt you;
Ever round your midnight bed
    Horrid sprites shall haunt you!'

'I'll wed another like my Dear
    Nancy, Nancy;
Then all hell will fly for fear,
    My spouse Nancy.'

Robert Burns

148   The Lass with a Lump of Land

Gi'e me a lass with a lump of land,
    And we for life shall gang the gither,
Though daft or wise, I'll never demand,
    Or black or fair, it maksna whether.
I'm aff with wit, and beauty will fade,
    And bloom alane is na worth a shilling;
But she that's rich, her market's made,
    For ilka charm about her is killing.

Gi'e me a lass with a lump of land,
    And in my bosom I'll hug my treasure;
Gin I had anes her gear in my hand,
    Should love turn dowf, it will find pleasure.
Laugh on wha likes, but there's my hand,
    I hate with poortith, though bonny, to meddle,
Unless they bring cash, or a lump of land,
    They'se never get me to dance to their fiddle.

There's meikle good love in bands and bags,
    And siller and gowd's a sweet complexion;
But beauty, and wit, and vertue in rags,
    Have tint the art of gaining affection:
Love tips his arrows with woods and parks,
    And castles, and riggs, and muirs, and meadows,
And naithing can catch our modern sparks,
    But well-tocher'd lasses, or jointur'd widows.

                                        Allan Ramsay

gi'e – give; gang the gither – go together; daft – foolish; maksna – does not matter;
ilka – every; gin – if; anes – once; gear – property; dowf – dull; poortith – poverty;
they'se – they'll; meikle – much; bands – bonds; siller – silver; gowd – gold; tint –
lost; parks – pastures; riggs – arable ridges; muirs – moors; tocher'd – dowered.

'O wha's that at my chamber door?', —
   'Fair widow, are ye wawking?'
'Auld carl, your suit give o'er,
   Your love lies a' in tawking.
Gi'e me a lad that's young and tight,
   Sweet like an April meadow;
'Tis sic as he can bless the sight
   And bosom of a widow.'

'O widow, wilt thou let me in,
   I'm pawky, wise, and thrifty,
And come of a right gentle kin,
   I'm little mair than fifty.'
'Daft carl, dit your mouth,
   What signifies how pawky,
Or gentle born ye be, — bot youth,
   In love you're but a gawky.'

Then, widow, let these guineas speak,
   That powerfully plead clinkan,
And if they fail, my mouth I'll steek,
   And nae mair love will think on.'
'These court indeed, I maun confess,
   I think they make you young, Sir,
And ten times better can express
   Affection, than your tongue, Sir.'

Allan Ramsay

wawking — waking; auld carl — old fellow; gi'e — give; tight — virile; sic — such;
pawky — crafty; dit — wipe; bot — without; gawky — booby; steek — close; mair —
more.

150   Tibbie Fowler o' the Glen

Tibbie Fowler o' the Glen,
   There's o'er mony wooin at her;
Tibbie Fowler o' the Glen,
   There's o'er mony wooin at her.

> *Wooin at her, pu'in at her,*
> *Courtin at her, canna get her:*
> *Filthy elf, it's for her pelf*
> *That a' the lads are wooin at her.*

Ten cam east, and ten cam west;
　Ten came rowin o'er the water;
Twa came down the lang dyke side,
　There's twa and thirty wooin at her.
Wooin at her, etc.

There's seven but, and seven ben,
　Seven in the pantry wi' her;
Twenty head about the door,
　There's ane-and-forty wooin at her.
Wooin at her, etc.

She's got pendles in her lugs,
　Cockle-shells wad set her better;
High-heel'd shoon and siller tags,
　And a' the lads are wooin at her.
Wooin at her, etc.

Be a lassie e'er sae black,
　An she hae the name o' siller,
Set her upo' Tintock-tap,
　The wind will blaw a man till her.
Wooin at her, etc.

Be a lassie e'er so fair,
　An she want the pennie siller,
A flie may fell her in the air,
　Before a man be even till her.
Wooin at her, etc.

Robert Burns

o'er mony – far too many; *canna* – can't; *cam* – came; *dyke* – ditch or wall; *but* – in the outer chamber; *ben* – in the inner chamber; *pendles* – ear-rings; *lugs* – ears; *shoon* – shoes; *tags* – fasteners; *black* – dark-haired; *gin* – if; *siller* – money; *Tintock* – Tinto Hill in Lanarkshire; *till* – to; *an* – if; *flie* – insect; *even till* – considered as a match for.

Chorus
An O, for ane and twenty, Tam!
And hey, sweet ane and twenty, Tam!
I'll learn my kin a rattlin sang,
An I saw ane and twenty, Tam.

They snool me sair, and haud me down,
    And gar me look like bluntie, Tam;
But three short years will soon wheel roun',
    And then comes ane and twenty, Tam.
        An O, for etc.

A gleib o' lan', a claut o' gear,
    Was left me by my Auntie, Tam;
At kith or kin I need na spier,
    An I saw ane and twenty, Tam.
        An O, for etc.

They'll hae me wed a wealthy coof,
    Tho' I mysel hae plenty, Tam;
But hearst thou, laddie, there's my loof,
    I'm thine at ane and twenty, Tam!
        An O, for etc.

                                        Robert Burns

rattlin — lively; *an* — if; *snool* — snub; *sair* — sorely; *haud* — hold; *gar* — to make;
bluntie — a fool; *gleib* — portion of land; *claut o' gear* — small amount of property;
spier — ask; *coof* — dolt; *loof* — palm.

152   Poortith cauld and restless Love

O poortith cauld , and restless love,
    Ye wrack my peace between ye;
Yet poortith a' I could forgive,
    An 'twere na for my Jeanie.

Chorus
O why should Fate sic pleasure have,
Life's dearest bands untwining?
Or why sae sweet a flower as love
Depend on Fortune's shining?

The warld's wealth when I think on,
   Its pride, and a' the lave o't;
My curse on silly coward man,
   That he should be the slave o't.
      O why, etc.

Her een sae bonie blue betray,
   How she repays my passion;
But Prudence is her o'erword ay,
   She talks o' rank and fashion.
      O why, etc.

O wha can prudence think upon,
   And sic a lassie by him:
O wha can prudence think upon,
   And sae in love as I am?
      O why, etc.

How blest the wild-wood Indian's fate,
   He woos his simple Dearie;
The silly bogles, Wealth and State,
   Did never make them eerie.
      O why, etc.

Robert Burns

poortith – poverty; *cauld* – cold; *a'* – all; *sic* – such; *sae* – so; *lave* – rest; *een* – eyes; *o'erword* – refrain; *aye* – always; *bogles* – goblins; *eerie* – afraid (of the supernatural).

153   Liberty preserved: or, Love destroyed

At length the bondage I have broke
    Which gave me so much pain;
I've slipt my heart out of the yoke,
    Never to drudge again;
And, conscious of my long disgrace,
Have thrown my chain at Cupid's face.

If ever he attempt again
    My freedom to enslave,
I'll court the Godhead of champagne
    Which makes the coward brave;
And, when that deity has heal'd my soul,
I'll drown the little Bastard in my bowl.

                    Alexander Robertson of Struan

154   My Love she's but a Lassie yet

        Chorus
My love she's but a lassie yet,
My love she's but a lassie yet;
We'll let her stand a year or twa,
She'll no be half sae saucy yet.

I rue the day I sought her O,
I rue the day I sought her O,
Wha gets her needs na say he's woo'd,
But he may say he's bought her O.
My love etc.

Come draw a drap o' the best o't yet,
Come draw a drap o' the best o't yet:
Gae seek for Pleasure whare ye will,
But here I never misst it yet.
My love etc.

We're a' dry wi' drinking o't,
We're a' dry wi' drinking o't;
The minister kisst the fidler's wife,
He could na preach for thinkin o't.
My love etc.

Robert Burns

sae – so; *na* – not; *drap o' the best o't* – drop of the best ale; *gae* – go; *a'* – all.

155   Gowf my Logie

Of modest maids in simple weeds,
   I've nothing for to say man,
But 'gainst the game of hawking wench,
   I'll tell you and you'll stay man.

Chorus
And ye busk sae bra lassie,
   And ye busk sae bra,
The lads will crack your maidenhead,
   And that's against the law.

I view them aft come to the church,
   With meal upon their hair man;
Whom I have seen in former times,
   With back and buttocks bare man;
O do not look so high lassie,
   O do not look so high,
You'll mind your mither was but poor,
   Though now ye drink your tea.

Those dirty maids come to the church,
   Holding their mouths so mim man,
Like riddle-rims their tails go round,
   Fine coats stript in the loom man;
O vow but ye be vogie lassie,
   O vow but ye be vogie,
You're proud to wear that whorelike coat,
   It's name is gowf my logie.

gowf – strike; *logie* – a hole before the fireplace in a kiln (i.e. a euphemism); *and* –
if; *busk* – dress; *aft* – often; *mim* – precise; *vow!* – interjection; *vogie* – vain.
Note – these are the first 24 lines of a satirical broadside similar in tone to No. 20,
above.

I am a poor, silly, auld man
And hirpling o'er a tree,
Yet fain, fain kiss wad I,
Gin the kirk wad let me be.

Gin a' my duds were aff
And a' hail claes on,
O, I could kiss a young lass,
As weel as can ony man!

hirpling – limping; *tree* – walking-stick; *gin* – if; *duds* – rags; *hail claes* – whole clothes.

157   The Fornicator

Ye jovial boys who love the joys,
    The blissful joys of Lovers;
Yet dare avow, with dauntless brow,
    When the bony lass discovers;
I pray draw near, and lend an ear,
    And welcome in a Frater,
For I've lately been on quarantine,
    A proven Fornicator.

Before the Congregation wide
    I pass'd the muster fairly,
My handsome Betsey by my side,
    We gat our ditty rarely;
But my downcast eye by chance did spy
    What made my lips to water,
Those limbs so clean where I, between,
    Commenc'd a Fornicator.

With rueful face and signs of grace
    I pay'd the buttock-hire,
But the night was dark and thro' the park
    I could not but convoy her;

A parting kiss, what could I less,
  My vows began to scatter,
My Betsey fell — lal de dal lal lal,
  I am a Fornicator.

But for her sake this vow I make,
  And solemnly I swear it,
That while I own a single crown
  She's welcome for to share it;
And my roguish boy his Mother's joy,
  And the darling of his Pater,
For him I boast my pains and cost,
  Although a Fornicator.

Ye wenching blades whose hireling jades
  Have tipt you off blue-boram,
I tell you plain, I do disdain
  To rank you in the Quorum;
But a bony lass upon the grass
  To teach her esse Mater,
And no reward but for regard,
  O that's a Fornicator.

Your warlike Kings and Heros bold,
  Great Captains and Commanders;
Your mighty Caesars fam'd of old,
  And Conquering Alexanders;
In fields they fought and laurels bought,
  And bulwarks strong did batter,
But still they grac'd our noble list,
  And ranked Fornicator!

Robert Burns

Before the Congregation — i.e. in public penance in Church; *Betsey* — Elizabeth
Paton; *gat our ditty* — received our reproof; *blue-boram* — the pox.

158   Godly Girzie

The night it was a haly night,
  The day had been a haly day;
Kilmarnock gleam'd wi' candle light,
  As Girzie hameward took her way.

A man o' sin, ill may he thrive!
   And never haly-meeting see!
Wi' godly Girzie met belyve,
   Amang the Cragie hills sae hie.

The chiel' was wight, the chiel' was stark,
   He wad na wait to chap nor ca',
And she was faint wi haly wark,
   She had na pith to say him na.
But ay she glowr'd up to the moon,
   And ay she sigh'd most piouslie;
'I trust my heart's in heaven aboon,
   Whare'er your sinfu' pintle be.'

Robert Burns

haly – holy; *belyve* – at once; *Cragie* – between Kilmarnock and Tarbolton; *hie* –
high; *chiel* – fellow; *wight* – stout; *stark* – strong; *chap* – knock; *ay* – always;
glowr'd – gazed; *aboon* – above; *pintle* – penis.

TABLE OF THE LYRICS AS PRINTED

Abbreviations

BM	British Museum
CLS 1748	*A Collection of Loyal Songs for the Use of the Revolution Club,* Edinburgh, 1748.
CLS 1750	*A Collection of Loyal Songs, Poems, etc. Printed in the Year 1750* (n. pl.).
Corri	*A New & Complete Collection of the Most Favorite Scots Songs . . . with Graces and Ornaments . . . By Signor Corri,* Edinburgh [1783].
Fergusson, S.T.S. edn.	*The Poems of Robert Fergusson,* ed. M.P. McDiarmid, Scottish Text Society, 1956.
Gunnyon, *Illustr.*	W. Gunnyon, *Illustrations of Scottish History, Life and Superstition from Song and Ballad,* Glasgow, 1879.
Hecht – Hd	*Songs from David Herd's Manuscripts,* ed. Hans Hecht, Edinburgh, 1904.
Herd, *Songs*	*Ancient and Modern Scottish Songs, Heroic Ballads, etc.,* 2 vols., Edinburgh, 1776. The 2nd, and fuller, edition of David Herd's printed collection.
Kinsley	*Burns: Poems and Songs,* ed. James Kinsley, London and Oxford, 1971.
St Clair MS.	A collection of Songs and Ballads made by Elizabeth St Clair between *c.* 1781 and *c.* 1785. Broughton House, Kirkcudbright.
MM	*The Merry Muses of Caledonia,* eds. James Barke and S. Goodsir Smith, Edinburgh, 1959.
NLS	National Library of Scotland.
OC	*Orpheus Caledonius: or, a Collection of Scots Songs Set to Musick by W. Thomson,* 2 vols., London, 1733.
SMM	*The Scots Musical Museum,* ed. James Johnson, 6 vols., Edinburgh, 1787-1803.

SN	*The Scots Nightingale: or, Edinburgh Vocal Miscellany,* Edinburgh, 1779.
Stenhouse, *Illustr.*	W. Stenhouse, *Notes and Illustrations* [to *The Scots Musical Museum*], Edinburgh, 1853.
TL	*The True Loyalist,* Edinburgh, 1779.
TTM	*The Tea-Table Miscellany,* ed. Allan Ramsay, 4 vols. Edinburgh, 1724-37. Texts have been collated with the edition of 1740, the earliest surviving edition to print the four volumes in one.
USS	*The Universal Scots Songster,* Edinburgh, 1781.
Wilkie MSS.	Thomas Wilkie, MS. Notebooks, 1813-15. NLS.

Note: Where the title of a volume is preceded by T (i.e. tune), this means that it contains the music for the lyric printed here.

1.	The Wren	Hecht — Hd; T Kinsley No. 524
2.	When I was a wee Thing	Hecht — Hd; T Kinsley No. 302
3.	The Nurse's Song	Hecht — Hd
4.	The Quaker's Wife	St Clair MS.; T Kinsley No. 408
5.	All in the Week's Work	St Clair MS.
6.	Jock and Meg	St Clair MS.
7.	Bonnyness and Pretty-ness	St Clair MS.; T Kinsley No. 350
8.	Bonny Ann	Wilkie MSS.; T Kinsley No. 80
9.	Willie Buckthorne	Wilkie MSS.
10.	Jacky Latin	St Clair MS.; T Kinsley No. 563
11.	I'd rather hae a Piece	St Clair MS.
12.	Cutty's Wedding	St Clair MS.
13.	Mally Lee	St Clair MS.
14.	The Tailor fell through the Bed	St Clair MS.; T Kinsley No. 286
15.	Tom o' Lin	St Clair MS.; T Kinsley No. 350
16.	Jenny's a' wet	St Clair MS.; T Kinsley No. 360
17.	Comin thro' the Rye	St Clair MS.; T Kinsley No. 360
18.	The Last Farewell and Lamentation of Mrs. McLeod	NLS Broadsides

48.	It was a' for our rightfu' King	Burns; T Kinsley No. 589
49.	The Pretender's Manifesto	A. Cockburn; St Clair MS.; T Kinsley No. 84 (p. 165)
50.	You're welcome, Charlie Ştewart	CLS 1750; T Kinsley No. 579
51.	Tho' Geordie reigns in Jamie's stead	CLS 1750
52.	O Brother Sandie, hear ye the News?	CLS 1748
53.	As I be ga'an up the Street	TL; T SMM No. 488
54.	O wow, Marget, are ye in?	Hecht – Hd; T SMM No. 522
55.	The Hunting of the Wren	Hecht – Hd
56.	The Tree of Liberty	attrib. Burns; Kinsley No. 625
57.	As I stood by yon roofless Tower	Burns; T Kinsley No. 555
58.	The terrors of God invading the Soul	R. Erskine, *Gospel Sonnets*, 1818
59.	O God of Bethel	M. Bruce, *Life and Works*, 1926
60.	The Hour of my Departure's come	M. Bruce, *Life and Works*, 1926
61.	A Prayer under the Pressure of violent Anguish	Burns; T Kinsley No. 15
62.	Winter: a Dirge	Burns; T Kinsley No. 10
63.	A Prayer in the Prospect of Death	Burns; T Kinsley No. 13
64.	Jocky fou, Jenny fain	TTM; T Kinsley No. 377
65.	In yon Garden fine an' gay	T SMM No. 563
66.	Mary Morison	Burns; T Kinsley No. 30
67.	Dunt, dunt, pittie, pattie	TTM; T SMM No. 122
68.	Wat and weary	Hecht – Hd; T Kinsley No. 287
69.	O my Love's bonny	Hecht – Hd; T SMM No. 594
70.	Slighted Nancy	Ramsay, TTM; T Kinsley No. 492
71.	Oh wert Thou in the cauld Blast	Burns; T Kinsley No. 524
72.	Some say that Kissing's a Sin	Herd, *Songs;* T Kinsley No. 277

INDEX OF FIRST LINES   169

INDEX OF KNOWN AUTHORS

The references are to the numbers of the poems